Oxford AQA GCSE History

Conflict and Tension:

The Inter-War Years

1918-1939

Revision Guide

 RECAP  APPLY REVIEW ✓ SUCCEED

Ellen Longley

SERIES EDITOR
Aaron Wilkes

OXFORD

Great Clarendon Street, Oxford, OX2 6DP, United Kingdom

Oxford University Press is a department of the University of Oxford.

It furthers the University's objective of excellence in research, scholarship, and education by publishing worldwide. Oxford is a registered trade mark of Oxford University Press in the UK and in certain other countries.

British Library Cataloguing in Publication Data

Data available

978-0-19-842291-4

Kindle edition 978-0-19-842292-1

10 9 8 7 6 5

Paper used in the production of this book is a natural, recyclable product made from wood grown in sustainable forests.

The manufacturing process conforms to the environmental regulations of the country of origin.

Printed in Italy by L.E.G.O. S.p.A. - Lavis - TN

Acknowledgements

The publisher would like to thank Jon Cloake for his work on the Student Book on which this Revision Guide is based, and Lindsay Bruce for reviewing this Revision Guide.

The publishers would like to thank the following for permissions to use their photographs:

Cover: Corbis UK Ltd/Getty Images

Photos: p12, p18 (M), p32, p39, p44 & p49 (BL): murat irfan yalcin/Shutterstock; **p13:** Chronicle Stock Photo/Alamy; **p19:** David Cohen Fine Art/Mary Evans Picture Library; **p18 (T), p32, p39, p44 & p49 (ML):** charnsitr/Shutterstock; **p21:** akg-images/Alamy; **p25 (T):** Daily Express; **p25 (B):** INTERFOTO/Alamy; **p27:** Muzzled; **p28:** AVS-Images/Shutterstock; **p32:** roihun matpor/Shutterstock; **p33:** Mary Evans Picture Library; **p37:** David Low/Solo Syndication; **p43:** David Low/Solo Syndication; **p45:** Mary Evans Picture Library; **p47:** Punch Cartoon Library; **p49 (TL):** Marco Rosales/Shutterstock; **p49 (TR):** Filip Bjorkman/Shutterstock; **p51:** Heritage Image Partnership Ltd / Alamy; **p53:** Strube/Daily Express/N&S Syndication; **p55:** Associated Newspapers Ltd./Solo Syndication; **p58:** David Low/Solo Syndication; **p59:** Wikipedia Commons

We are grateful for permission to include the following copyright material:

General Ismay: from a memo to the British Cabinet, 20 Sept 1938, used by permission of The National Archives.

Adolf Hitler: *Mein Kampf* translated by Ralph Manheim (Hutchinson 1969, Pimlico 1992), translation copyright © 1943, used by permission of The Random House Group Ltd.

Fridjhof Nansen: from the presentation speech given at the Nobel Peace Prize Ceremony in 1926, copyright © The Nobel Foundation, used by permission of The Nobel Foundation.

Although we have made every effort to trace and contact all copyright holders before publication this has not been possible in all cases. If notified, the publisher will rectify any errors or omissions at the earliest opportunity.

Links to third party websites are provided by Oxford in good faith and for information only. Oxford disclaims any responsibility for the materials contained in any third party website referenced in this work.

Contents

RECAP **APPLY** **REVIEW**

Part one:

Peacemaking

1 The armistice   **12**

2 The Versailles Settlement   **14**

3 Impact of the treaty and wider settlement   **16**

Part two:

The League of Nations and international peace

4 The League of Nations   **26**

5 Diplomacy outside the League   **32**

6 The collapse of the League   **34**

Contents

RECAP   **APPLY**   **REVIEW**

Part three:

The origins and outbreak of the Second World War

Introduction

The *Oxford AQA GCSE History* textbook series has been developed by an expert team led by Jon Cloake and Aaron Wilkes. This matching Revision Guide offers you step-by-step strategies to master your AQA Wider World Depth Study: Conflict and Tension exam skills, and the structured revision approach of **Recap, Apply and Review** to prepare you for exam success.

Use the checklists on pages 3–4 to keep track of your revision, and use the traffic light feature on each page to monitor your confidence level on each topic. Other exam practice and revision features include Top revision tips on page 6, and the 'How to...' guides for each exam question type on pages 7–9.

 RECAP Each chapter recaps key events and developments through easy-to-digest chunks and visual diagrams. **Key terms** appear in bold and red; they are defined in the glossary. indicates the relevant Oxford AQA History Student Book pages so you could easily re-read the textbook for further revision.

SUMMARY highlights the most important facts at the end of each chapter.

TIMELINE provides a short list of dates to help you remember key events.

APPLY Each revision activity is designed to help drill your understanding of facts, and then progress towards applying your knowledge to exam questions.

These targeted revision activities are written specifically for this guide, which will help you apply your knowledge towards the four exam questions in your AQA Conflict and Tension exam paper:

SOURCE ANALYSIS   **HOW FAR DO YOU AGREE?**   **WRITE AN ACCOUNT**

 Examiner Tip highlights key parts of an exam question, and gives you hints on how to avoid common mistakes in exams.

 Revision Skills provides different revision techniques. Research shows that using a variety of revision styles can help cement your revision.

 Review gives you helpful reminders about how to check your answers and how to revise further.

 REVIEW Throughout each chapter, you can review and reflect on the work you have done, and find advice on how to further refresh your knowledge.

You can tick off the Review column from the progress checklist as you work through this Revision Guide. **Activity answers guidance** and the **Exam practice** sections with full sample student answers also help you to review your own work.

Top revision tips

Getting your revision right

It is perfectly natural to feel anxious when exam time approaches. The best way to keep on top of the stress is to be organised!

3 months to go

Plan: create a realistic revision timetable, and stick to it!

Track your progress: use the Progress Checklists (pages 3–4) to help you track your revision. It will help you stick to your revision plan.

Be realistic: revise in regular, small chunks, of around 30 minutes. Reward yourself with 10 minute breaks – you will be amazed how much more you'll remember.

Positive thinking: motivate yourself by turning your negative thoughts to positive ones. Instead of asking *'why can't I remember this topic at all?'* ask yourself *'what different techniques can I try to improve my memory?'*

Organise: make sure you have everything you need – your revision books, coloured pens, index cards, sticky notes, paper, etc. Find a quiet place where you are comfortable. Divide your notes into sections that are easy to use.

Timeline: create a timeline with colour-coded sticky notes, to make sure you remember important dates relating to the three parts of the Germany period study (use the Timeline on page 11 as a starting point).

Practise: ask your teachers for practice questions or past papers.

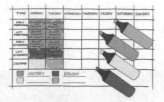

Revision techniques

Using a variety of revision techniques can help you remember information, so try out different methods:

- Make **flashcards**, using both sides of the card to test yourself on key figures, dates, and definitions
- **Colour-code** your notebooks
- **Reread** your textbook or copy out your notes
- Create **mind-maps** for complicated topics
- Draw **pictures** and symbols that spring to mind
- Group study
- Find a **buddy** or group to revise with and test you
- Listen to revision **podcasts** or watch revision **clips**
- Work through the **revision activities** in this guide.

Revision tips to help you pass your Conflict and Tension exam

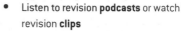

1 month to go

Key concepts: make sure you understand key concepts for this topic, such as the armistice, peace treaties, international cooperation, peace, tension, economic depression, appeasement and Communism. If you're unsure, attend your school revision sessions and ask your teacher to go through the concept again.

Identify your weaknesses: which topics or question types are easier and which are more challenging for you? Schedule more time to revise the challenging topics or question types.

Make it stick: find memorable ways to remember chronology, using fun rhymes, or doodles, for example.

Take a break: do something completely different during breaks – listen to music, take a short walk, make a cup of tea, for example.

Check your answers: answer the exam questions in this guide, then check the Activity answers guidance at the end of the guide to practise applying your knowledge to exam questions.

Understand your mark scheme: review the Mark scheme (page 10) for each exam question, and make sure you understand how you will be marked.

Master your exam skills: study and remember the How to master your exam skills steps (pages 7–9) for each AQA question type – it will help you plan your answers quickly!

Time yourself: practise making plans and answering exam questions within the recommended time limits.

Take mock exams seriously: you can learn from them how to manage your time better under exam conditions.

Rest well: make sure your phone and laptop are put away at least an hour before bed. This will help you rest better.

On the big day

Sleep early: Don't work through the night, get a good night's sleep.

Be prepared: Make sure you know where and when the exam is, and leave plenty of time to get there.

Check: make sure you have all your equipment in advance, including spare pens!

Drink and eat healthily: avoid too much caffeine or junk food. Water is best – if you are 5% dehydrated, then your concentration drops 20%.

Stay focused: don't listen to people who might try to wind you up about what might come up in the exam – they don't know any more than you.

Good luck!

Master your exam skills

Get to grips with your Paper 1: Conflict and Tension 1918–1939 Wider World Depth Study

The Paper 1 exam lasts 2 hours, and you must answer 10 questions covering 2 topics. The first 6 questions (worth 40 marks) will cover your Period Study (Germany, Russia, America 1840–1895 or America 1920–1973). The last 4 questions will cover Conflict and Tension. Here you will find details about what to expect with the last 4 questions relating to Conflict and Tension 1918–1939, and advice on how to master your exam skills.

▼ **SOURCE A**

▼ **SOURCE B**

▼ **SOURCE C**

1   Study **Source A. Source A** supports/opposes… How do you know? Explain your answer using **Source A** and your contextual knowledge.   [4 marks]

2   Study **Sources B** and **C**. How useful are **Sources B** and **C** to a historian studying… ? Explain your answer using **Sources B** and **C** and your own knowledge.   [12 marks]

3   Write an account of how…   [8 marks]

4   '…'
    How far do you agree with this statement? Explain your answer.
          [16 marks] [SPaG 4 marks]

REVISION SKILLS

Read the Period Study Revision Guide for help on the first 6 questions of Paper 1.

EXAMINER TIP

Don't forget to read the provenance (caption) for any sources you are given. It will give you valuable information and help you place the source in its historical context. You will be able to analyse what the source is saying (Question 1) and assess its value (usefulness) to the historian (Question 2).

EXAMINER TIP

Don't forget that you get up to 4 marks for spelling, punctuation and grammar (SPaG) on this question too.

REVIEW

Throughout this Revision Guide you will find activities that help you prepare for each type of question. They will help you recognise what a good answer looks like and how to develop your ideas to get a good level. Look out for the **REVISION SKILLS** tips too, to inspire you to find the revision strategies that work for you!

EXAMINER TIP

Don't forget you will also have to answer six questions relating to your Period Study in Paper 1. Ensure you leave enough time to complete both sections of Paper 1! You are advised to spend 50 minutes on your Period Study in the exam.

How to master source questions

Here are the steps to consider when answering the question that asks you how you know the opinion of a source.

Content

Look at the source carefully. You could label what you can see, or circle anything that you think is important. This might help you to break the source down and work out what it is about.

Provenance

Look at the date and other information in the source caption. The caption will give you a clue about what event(s)/issue/topic it is about. Think carefully about the events you have studied. Which one is the source about?

Context

Think back over your own knowledge. What features of the source content or provenance fit with what you know about the statement given in the question (such as 'Source D opposes or supports something')? What historical facts can you use to support your answer?

Comment

Make sure you use your own knowledge and information from the source to explain how the statement given in the question (such as 'Source D opposes or supports something') is shown.

 Spend about 5 minutes on this 4-mark question.

EXAMINER TIP

Try to describe at least one part of the source that either praises or criticises the event/person, then explain how this symbolises the statement in the question.

How to master 'how useful are the sources' questions

Remember that this question is similar to the source question in Paper 2, but this focuses on *two* sources.

Content

Read both sources and underline or circle any detail that helps you to work out what they are about.

Provenance

Next, look at the provenance for each source; is there anything about the Time, Author, Purpose, Audience or Site (place it was created) (TAPAS!) that makes the source more or less useful?

Context

Now think back over your own knowledge. For each source, write about whether the content and caption fit with what you know. Does it give a fair reflection of the person, event or issue it describes?

Comment

You now need to make a judgement about how useful each source is. Try to use the sources together. What could a historian use them to find out about?

For each source, make sure you explain what is suggested by the content – and link this to your own knowledge to explain your ideas. You should also explain how the provenance makes the source useful (or not!).

 This question is worth 12 marks. Spend around 15 minutes on it.

EXAMINER TIP

Don't forget that every source is useful for something. Don't start telling the examiner what you can't use the sources for; no source will tell you everything, so just focus on what it *does* say.

How to master 'write an account' questions

Here are the steps to consider for answering the 'write an account' question. This question involves telling the key moments of an event in relation to the topic of the question. You need to describe, explain and analyse how one development led to another.

Select the key moments

What will you include in your story? Spend 1 minute to work out 3–4 key moments that are *relevant* to the question. Make sure you organise the moments in chronological order (starting with the earliest). You must include 1–2 specific historical facts for each key moment and plenty of specific historical detail.

Explain the connections

Write your answer based on the key moments you identified, and explain how the moments connect together to cause the event to develop. Make sure you link the story to the point of the question. A top level answer will also include an explanation of how the tension rises with each event.

 Spend around 10 minutes on this 8-mark question, but remember that this needs to include planning time.

EXAMINER TIP

Use phrases such as 'this led to…' and 'as a result of this…' to help you link back to the question and keep your ideas focused.

How to master 'how far do you agree' questions

Read the question carefully

What statement is the question asking you to consider? The statement is located within the quotation marks. Underline key words in the statement to help you focus your answer.

Plan your essay

You could plan your essay by listing other reasons that caused the event/issue:

Stated reason 1	Another reason 2	Another reason 3

Write in anything you could use as evidence for the different reasons, but remember that you only have about 2–3 minutes to plan and 15–17 minutes to write your paragraphs. For each reason, choose 2 historical facts you are most confident about and highlight these.

Context

Now that you have planned which reasons to discuss, start writing your answer, which needs to link to your knowledge as well. Aim for about 4–5 paragraphs: 1 or 2 that explain the reason named in the question and your own facts to back up the statement, 2 that explain 2 other reasons and facts to back them up, and a conclusion that explains your overall judgment.

Conclude

This question asks you 'how far…' you agree with the statement, so make sure you come to a clear conclusion.

Check your SPaG

Don't forget that you get up to 4 marks for your SPaG in this answer. It's a good idea to leave time to check your SPaG.

 This question is worth 16 marks. Spend around 20 minutes on it, but this needs to include time to plan and to check your SPaG.

EXAMINER TIP

Make sure you keep your ideas focused; use facts you know to support your ideas and use the wording from the question to make sure you explain how each reason led to the event.

EXAMINER TIP

If you want to achieve Level 4, you will have to reach an overall judgement. Is there one reason that you think is definitely more important than the others? Why?

AQA GCSE History mark schemes

Below are simplified versions of the AQA mark schemes, to help you understand the marking criteria for your **Paper 1: Conflict and Tension** exam.

Level	Source question 1
2	• Developed analysis of source based on content and/or provenance • Relevant facts and reasoning are shown [3–4 marks]
1	• Simple analysis of source based on content and/or provenance • Some related facts are shown [1–2 marks]

Level	Sources question 2
4	• Complex evaluation of the 2 sources • Argument about how useful the sources are is shown throughout the answer, supported by evidence from provenance and content, and relevant facts [10–12 marks]
3	• Developed evaluation of the 2 sources • Argument is stated about how useful the sources are, supported by evidence from source content and/or provenance [7–9 marks]
2	• Simple evaluation of 1 or 2 sources • Argument about how useful the source(s) are is shown, based on content and/or provenance [4–6 marks]
1	• Basic analysis of 1 or 2 sources • Basic description of the source is shown [1–3 marks]

Level	'Write an account' question
4	• A well-developed answer, clearly structured and explained • Explains different stages that led to the crisis • May explain how tension rises at each stage or how each stage linked/led to the next [7–8 marks]
3	• A developed answer, well-structured and using a range of factual information to explain causes and/or consequences • Answer is supported by relevant facts/ understanding [5–6 marks]

2	• A simple, structured answer, using specific factual information to describe at least one cause or consequence [3–4 marks]
1	• Identifies causes and/or consequences of the event [1–2 marks]

Level	'How far do you agree' question
4	• Complex explanation of the reason named in the question and other reasons • Argument is shown throughout the structured answer, supported by a range of accurate, detailed and relevant facts [13–16 marks]
3	• Developed explanation of the reason named in the question and other factors • Argument is shown throughout the structured answer, supported by a range of accurate and relevant facts [9–12 marks]
2	• Simple explanation of one or more reasons • Argument is shown, supported by relevant facts [5–8 marks]
1	• Basic explanation of one or more reasons • Some basic facts are shown [1–4 marks]

You also achieve up to 4 marks for spelling, punctuation and grammar (SPaG) on the statement question:

Level	'How far do you agree' question SPaG marks
Excellent	• SPaG is accurate throughout the answer • Meaning is very clear • A *wide* range of key historical terms are used accurately [4 marks]
Good	• SPaG shown with considerable accuracy • Meaning is generally clear • A range of key historical terms are used [2–3 marks]
Satisfactory	• SPaG shown with some accuracy • SPaG allows historical understanding to be shown • Basic historical terms are used [1 mark]

Conflict and Tension, 1918–1939 Timeline

The colours represent different types of event as follows:

 Blue: economic events   Red: political events

 Black: international events or foreign policies

1918 **11 November** – the Armistice is signed, ending the First World War

1919 **June** – the Treaty of Versailles is signed

1921 Poland invades Vilna; the Aaland Islands crisis

1923 **August** – the Corfu crisis

1925 **October** – the Greek-Bulgarian dispute

 October-December – the Locarno Treaties

1929 **October** – the Wall Street Crash leads to global depression

1931 **September** – the Mukden Incident; the Japanese army invades Manchuria

1933 **January** – Hitler becomes Chancellor of Germany

 October – Hitler leaves the Disarmament Conference

1934 **July** – the Nazi Party in Austria assassinates the Austrian Chancellor, Dollfuss

1935 **January** – the Saar Plebiscite

 March – Hitler announces that he has built up the Luftwaffe and that conscription will be introduced to build up the German army

 June – the Anglo-German Naval Treaty

 October – Mussolini invades Abyssinia

1936 **March** – remilitarisation of the Rhineland

 October – the Rome-Berlin Axis is agreed

 November – the Anti-Comintern Pact between Germany and Japan is agreed

1938 **March** – Hitler invades Austria to achieve Anschluss

 September – Chamberlain meets Hitler to discuss the Sudeten crisis

 October – German troops invade and occupy the Sudetenland

1939 **August** – the Nazi-Soviet Pact is signed

 September – Hitler invades Poland; Britain and France declare war on Germany

CHAPTER 1

The armistice

The end of the First World War

The First World War was fought from 1914 to 1918 and was the bloodiest war the world had ever seen. At the end of the war the Germans surrendered and signed an **armistice** saying that they would:

- pay **reparations**

- give Alsace-Lorraine back to France

- move the German army out of the Rhineland.

The aims of the peacekeepers

In January 1919, 32 countries met in the Palace of Versailles to decide the terms of the final peace treaties. This became known as the **Paris Peace Conference**.

The discussions were led by **the 'Big Three'**: **David Lloyd George**, Prime Minister of Britain, **Georges Clemenceau**, Prime Minister of France, and **Woodrow Wilson**, President of the USA. There was a great deal of pressure on these leaders; they had to make a peace that would keep everyone happy, but Europe was falling apart so they needed to act quickly.

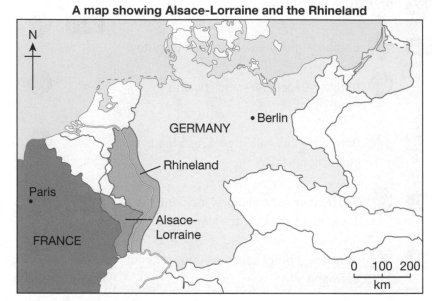

A map showing Alsace-Lorraine and the Rhineland

Leader	Country	Aims
Georges Clemenceau	France	• Wanted Germany to pay for reparations to rebuild areas of France badly affected by war • Wanted revenge for all the lives lost • Aimed to weaken Germany so it could never attack again • Wanted to push German border back to the Rhine so French people would feel safer
David Lloyd George	Britain	• Wanted a cautious approach: British public wanted Germany to be punished, but Lloyd George feared this would lead to Germany wanting revenge • Wanted to keep Germany strong so it could trade with Britain and act as a buffer to Communism • Aimed to gain German colonies to add to the British **Empire** • Wanted naval supremacy by reducing Germany's navy
Woodrow Wilson	USA	• Wanted a fair peace, so Germany would not seek revenge • Proposed the **Fourteen Points**, including foundation of a **League of Nations**, **self-determination** and freedom of the seas; but the American public didn't want the USA to get involved in European affairs again

SUMMARY

- The Big Three met at the Paris Peace Conference to agree the **Treaty** of Versailles.
- Each man wanted to achieve different things, and each nation put pressure on their leader to get what they wanted.
- The Big Three had to act quickly as Europe was unstable after the war.

 **APPLY**

WRITE AN ACCOUNT

Make a set of four flashcards, summarising the key points of the armistice and the aims of each of the Big Three.

EXAMINER TIP

Your flashcards can help prepare you for answering exam questions such as: 'Write an account of why the Big Three disagreed at the Treaty of Versailles.'

SOURCE ANALYSIS

▶ **SOURCE A** *The front cover of a French magazine from 1919; the tiger represents Clemenceau and the tiger's prey is an eagle, a symbol of Germany*

a Read the exam question below and circle the key words that tell you what you need to do. For example, you should circle 'opposes' as it tells you what the cartoonist's opinion is, and what you need to find supporting evidence for.

> **EXAM QUESTION** **Source A** opposes Clemenceau and his aims at the Paris Peace Conference. How do you know? Explain your answer using **Source A** and your contextual knowledge.

b Use the writing frame below to help you plan an answer to this exam question.

First, use the source to explain how you know that the creator's opinion of Clemenceau is negative. What symbolism is used?	_____ _____ _____ _____
Now, use your own knowledge to explain why some people felt like this. What did Clemenceau want that was so 'fierce'?	_____ _____ _____ _____

EXAMINER TIP

You should spend about five minutes on the source question. Plan your time carefully in the exam — make sure you leave enough time for the longer essay questions.

The Versailles Settlement

The terms of the treaty

- The Treaty of Versailles was signed on 28 June 1919.

- The final treaty was a **Diktat** – Germany was not allowed to negotiate the terms.

- The Germans were devastated by the final terms, and the Big Three weren't really satisfied either.

These were the terms Germany had to agree to:

Article 231: the war guilt clause		Danzig was taken from Germany	
Article 232: reparations – the amount was set at £6,600 million in 1921		The German army was limited to 100,000 men	
German navy restricted to 15,000 men, with only 1500 officers		Germany was split in two by the Polish Corridor	
Anschluss was forbidden		**Conscription** was not allowed	
The German navy was only allowed six battleships		The Saar was given to the League of Nations to control for 15 years	
The League of Nations was formed, but Germany could not join		The Rhineland was **demilitarised**	
Germany was not allowed tanks, submarines or an air force		Germany's colonies were given to the League of Nations as **mandates**	

SUMMARY

- No one was really satisfied with the Treaty of Versailles.

- The Germans felt that it was unfairly harsh, and that the military, territorial and economic terms they faced would ruin them.

APPLY

HOW FAR DO YOU AGREE?

In the exam you might get asked a question about what Germany lost in the terms of the Treaty of Versailles. Start thinking about how you would answer this kind of question by categorising each of the terms in the table opposite. Next to each one, draw a symbol or symbols to represent what Germany lost – the first few have been done for you. Choose from the following:

 represents damage to pride

 represents economic damage

 represents military loss

 represents territorial loss

Remember, some terms might be evidence of Germany losing more than one thing.

HOW FAR DO YOU AGREE?

Use the planning grid below to plan your answer to the following exam question, before having a go at it.

 EXAM QUESTION 'Reparations were the worst punishment imposed on Germany in the Treaty of Versailles.' How far do you agree with this statement? Explain your answer.

Introduction: Start off with your overall judgement: write this in the box to the right to help you focus on it throughout your answer.			
	Point:	**Evidence:**	**Explanation** (how did this affect the people of Germany?):
Agree with the statement by explaining the impact reparations had on Germany.	Why Germany hated reparations		
Disagree with the statement by considering how else Germany was affected.	Other terms: Territory		
	Other terms: Military		
Conclusion: Come back to your overall judgement, but try to make a new point, don't just sum up what you've already said. For example, you could explain how one term led to others, or how one term made the others worse.			

 EXAMINER TIP

Lots of students are good at describing the different terms, but not as good at explaining their impact. Make sure you link your points back to the question using a sentence like 'this was a terrible punishment for Germany because …'. Make sure you explain what the impact on Germany was – how did affect people living there?

 EXAMINER TIP

Make sure you leave enough time to write your essay in the exam. An essay answer should probably take you no more than 20 minutes.

 EXAMINER TIP

Don't forget you get up to four marks for spelling, punctuation and grammar on this question: make sure you write in paragraphs, use capital letters for proper nouns, and check your answer carefully at the end. If you can use historical words (like the ones in red throughout this book) correctly, you may get higher SPaG marks.

CHAPTER 3

Impact of the treaty and wider settlement

RECAP

Did the Big Three achieve their aims?

Each of the Big Three had different aims, and all of them achieved some of them – but how happy were they overall?

Georges Clemenceau

Clemenceau was pleased about:

- France gaining Alsace-Lorraine
- Germany having no army present in the Rhineland

Clemenceau was unhappy about:

- the reparations: the French thought Germany should pay more
- Germany being allowed to have an army, even a small one
- the Rhineland not being completely taken away from Germany

David Lloyd George

Lloyd George was pleased about:

- Britain having naval supremacy over Germany
- the British Empire gaining more colonies

Lloyd George was unhappy about:

- the harsh reparations meaning Britain would lose trade with Germany
- the threat of a possible future war as the Germans were so unhappy

Woodrow Wilson

Wilson was pleased about:

- the creation of the League of Nations

Wilson was unhappy about:

- the Fourteen Points being ignored in the treaty terms
- the harshness of the treaty terms

Why couldn't the Big Three get everything they wanted?

- Europe was crumbling after the war so the Big Three were under pressure to reach an agreement quickly. The Austro-Hungarian and Ottoman empires had collapsed, leaving countries without stable governments. Each politician had to do what the people of their country wanted, to get re-elected. The ordinary citizens had been fed anti-German **propaganda** during the war and felt little mercy towards the losers.

- Wilson wanted the USA to join the League of Nations, but the US Senate followed a policy of **isolationism** and refused this.

- Wilson and Lloyd George now disagreed over the original terms of the armistice that Germany had signed in November 1918.

- During the war, countries had been promised rewards for joining on the side of the Allies, for example Italy was promised land. The Big Three had to keep these promises, even if they weren't in everyone's best interests.

- The Big Three each had different and often contrasting aims – they had to compromise.

 **APPLY**

HOW FAR DO YOU AGREE?

a Look carefully at the terms each of the Big Three were happy and unhappy about. Rank each of the Big Three along an opinion line, in order of who you think was most and least satisfied with the terms of the Treaty of Versailles. Write a paragraph to explain the order you have chosen.

b Look at the list of reasons the Big Three could not achieve everything they wanted to. Which do you think were the three most important? Write them out in order of importance.

c Create a 10-point fact sheet to test detailed knowledge about the Treaty of Versailles. You could swap this with a friend to see if you have selected the same facts. Be prepared to justify why you have chosen your facts.

d
> **EXAM QUESTION** 'The main reason the Big Three were dissatisfied with the Treaty of Versailles was because they had to compromise with each other.' How far do you agree with this statement? Explain your answer.

EXAMINER TIP

Always work out what the different sides of your answer will be. Here, you need to consider how the different aims of the Big Three meant that they could not get what they wanted, but you also need to think about the other reasons they were never going to be fully happy with the final treaty.

How did the Allies react to the Treaty of Versailles?

Of course, it wasn't just the Big Three who had to be satisfied with the final treaty. Did the treaty please the people back home?

Britain

Propaganda during the war taught the Brits to despise the Germans, and lots of British soldiers had been killed in the war.

British people generally thought that the treaty was fair, and could even have been harsher.

Lloyd George was hailed as a hero, and newspapers said Britain would never be threatened by Germany again.

France

Many people in France were furious – they believed that the treaty was nowhere near harsh enough and that Germany should suffer as much as France had during the war.

People felt Clemenceau had not done enough to get revenge for France and he was voted out in the next election.

There were a few terms that the people of France liked, such as gaining control of the Saar and its coalfields for 15 years.

USA

The USA had only joined the war in 1917 and no fighting took place on US soil, so Americans did not want revenge or compensation in the same way that the British and French did.

Many people felt that the treaty was too harsh, including Wilson.

The USA wanted to follow a policy of isolationism.

The US Senate refused to approve the treaty or to allow the USA to join the League of Nations.

REVISION SKILLS

Break down the information for a topic in different ways. You can create a brief fact file, a bit like the boxes above, containing two or three important points about the country, person or event concerned.

 APPLY

SOURCE ANALYSIS

◀ **SOURCE A** *A plate made to commemorate the signing of the Treaty of Versailles*

Look at **Source A.** Which country do you think this plate was made in? Explain your answer using details from the source linked to your own knowledge.

SOURCE ANALYSIS

▼ **SOURCE B** *Adapted from John Maynard Keynes, a British economist, in his book The Economic Consequences of Peace, 1920; he was at the Paris Peace Conference:*

> The treaty includes no solutions for the economic rehabilitation of Europe – nothing to make the defeated central empires into good neighbours, nothing to stabilise the new states of Europe ... nor does it promote in any way an agreement of economic solidarity among the Allies themselves; no arrangement was reached at Paris for restoring the disordered finances of France.

In the exam you will be asked how useful two sources are to a historian studying a certain issue. In this activity you will build up the skills you need to analyse sources and answer the following question, but concentrating on just one source for now:

EXAM QUESTION How useful is **Source B** to a historian studying the reasons why the Big Three were not satisfied with the Treaty of Versailles?

a First work out what the source is useful for. Find evidence from the source that describes why people criticised the Treaty of Versailles; you might want to highlight or underline each criticism in the source. Complete the table below to help you organise your ideas:

Criticism	Who felt this way?	Why did people feel like this?
No solutions for the economic rehabilitation of Europe	David Lloyd George	Concerned that heavy reparations would mean Germany and Britain could not trade

b Now think about the provenance of **Source B**. How does this make the source useful to a historian studying why people criticised the treaty?

c Use your ideas from parts **a** and **b** to help you answer the exam question above.

EXAMINER TIP

When asked how useful sources are, try to be positive. Assume that the source is useful and avoid listing what it does not cover. Demonstrate to the examiner that you understand what the source is saying and why people at the time felt this way. You could also consider the provenance (information about the source such as who wrote it and when) and how this makes the source useful to a historian.

REVIEW

To remind yourself of the Big Three's aims when agreeing the Treaty of Versailles, look back to Chapter 1, pages 12–13.

German objections to the Treaty of Versailles

The war guilt clause, meaning Germany accepted responsibility for starting the war, was particularly hated

The German people felt the treaty was forced on them and they were not allowed to negotiate the terms. They called it a 'Diktat', meaning 'dictated peace'

They had been told they were winning the war, so felt they had been stabbed in the back and betrayed by the government. People called those who had signed the armistice the **November Criminals**

13% of land was lost to other countries so six million German people found that they were no longer living in Germany

Why did German people hate the treaty so much?

The people were starving because Britain had blockaded the German ports during the war, so little food had been imported into Germany. They were desperate and needed help; they did not see how they could cope with the punishments they were facing

The German people felt it left them vulnerable – they were hated by their old enemies and without a large army to defend them they could be attacked easily

The Kaiser (German king) had been forced to **abdicate** before the treaty was signed, so there was uncertainty about how the country would be run. People also felt that the person who was responsible for the war (the Kaiser) had been punished, so there was no need for further punishment

Timeline: Impacts of the Treaty of Versailles

▼ 1920

- The Kapp Putsch – an attempted revolution in Germany

Vile Versailles!

▼ 1921

- Reparations set at £6,600 million

▼ 1923

- January: The Ruhr crisis – France invades Germany to take goods from factories when Germany fails to make a reparations payment; the German government pays workers to strike (so there are no goods for the French to take) and prints off more banknotes to pay them, leading to **hyperinflation**

- November: the Munich Putsch

Price: 201,000,000,000 marks

▼ 1924

- USA lends Germany 800 million gold marks in the Dawes Plan

APPLY

SOURCE ANALYSIS

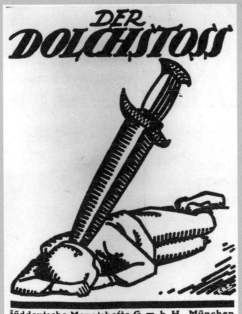

DER DOLCHSTOSS

Süddeutsche Monatshefte G. m. b. H., München
Preis Goldmark 1.10.

◀ **SOURCE A** *From a history book published in Germany in 1924*

a Summarise the reasons German people felt they had been treated unfairly in the Treaty of Versailles.

b How did the reparations affect Germany? Try to give examples of the short- and long-term impacts.

c EXAM QUESTION **Source** A criticises the German politicians who accepted the Treaty of Versailles. How do you know? Explain your answer using **Source A** and your contextual knowledge.

EXAMINER TIP

First, work out what the source shows. Labelling a couple of the key features might help you to do this in the exam. Then, link these images to what you know about the event. Does the picture link to a specific reason many people in Germany hated the treaty?

HOW FAR DO YOU AGREE?

 EXAM QUESTION 'The main reason why Germany hated the Treaty of Versailles was because of its financial terms.' How far do you agree with this statement? Explain your answer.

How were Germany's allies treated at the end of the war?

Germany had fought along with other countries during the First World War, so the peacemakers also had to decide how to treat Germany's allies. The table below outlines what was decided:

Country:	Austria	Bulgaria	Hungary	Turkey
Name of treaty:	Treaty of St Germain	Treaty of Neuilly	Treaty of Trianon	Treaty of Sèvres
Date:	10 September 1919	27 November 1919	4 June 1920	10 August 1920
Land:	Land taken to create new countries Czechoslovakia and Yugoslavia	Lost land to Yugoslavia and Greece	Lost land to Romania, Czechoslovakia, Yugoslavia and Austria	Split up the Turkish Empire so Turkey lost nearly all its land in Europe
Reparations:	Agreed in principal, but the amount was never fixed	£100 million	Agreed in principal, but the amount was never fixed	None
Military restrictions:	30,000 in army; no conscriptions; no navy	20,000 in army; no conscriptions; no air force; only four battleships	30,000 in army; no conscription; only three patrol boats	50,000 in army; seven sailboats; six torpedo boats
Other terms:	Forbidden to unite with Germany	None	None	Dardanelles and Bosphorus straits were opened to other countries

Impact of the treaties and problems faced by new states

- Losing land meant the Austrian and Hungarian economies collapsed in 1921.

- People in Turkey revolted over the Treaty of Sèvres, so the British replaced it with the **Treaty of Lausanne** in July 1923. This was hugely symbolic as it proved that the treaties could not be enforced and showed that Britain was willing to undermine the treaties.

- Rather than being controlled by the Austro-Hungarian Empire, east Europe was now divided into lots of small countries.

- Poland was created from land previously owned by Germany, but this caused lots of problems:

  - Germans living in the new country were unhappy and Russia argued about Poland's eastern borders.

  - Poland had no natural borders, such as mountains or rivers, so it could not be defended easily.

- Germany was split by the **Polish Corridor** — a strip of land that gave Poland access to the sea. This meant that Poland now owned land where German people lived, who were not happy to find that they now had a new nationality. Germany was also split in two, which weakened it and caused much resentment towards Poland.

Europe before 1919

Europe after 1919

⚙ APPLY

HOW FAR DO YOU AGREE?

EXAM QUESTION 'The loss of land to create new countries was the main reason for the dissatisfaction of Germany's allies with the peacemakers, 1919 to 1920.' How far do you agree with this statement? Explain your answer.

a Who lost most in the treaties agreed at the end of the First World War? Think carefully about what Germany, Austria, Bulgaria, Hungary and Turkey lost and what the impacts were. Write the country names in the top row of boxes below in order, from the most badly affected to the least.

most badly affected   **least badly affected**

b Explain why you decided on this order. Under each country, in the second row of boxes, write a brief explanation of the impact the treaties had on each country.

c Have a go at the exam question above.

WRITE AN ACCOUNT

a Write a one- or two-sentence summary of the problems that each of the treaties signed at the end of the First World War caused.

b **EXAM QUESTION** Write an account of how the Treaty of Sèvres led to an international crisis.

 **RECAP**

Assessing the Treaty of Versailles

Ever since the peace treaties were created, there have been strong views about the strengths and weaknesses of them. Some people argue that the treaties were fair and sensible and that the peacemakers did the best they could under difficult circumstances. Others argue that the treaties simply created more problems than they solved.

Strengths

- The war had caused huge amounts of damage, especially in France, so the reparations were needed to rebuild.

- France regained Alsace-Lorraine.

- Many areas had not wanted to be part of the Austro-Hungarian Empire. Places like Czechoslovakia and Poland were now given independence.

Weaknesses

- New states were created, but Poland was weakened because it was surrounded by enemies with borders that were difficult to defend.

- Austria and Hungary lost so much land that their economies crashed in 1921.

- Lloyd George and Wilson feared that the treaties would lead to another war in the future.

- The Treaty of Lausanne proved that the treaties could not be enforced and showed people like Hitler and Mussolini that Britain was willing to undermine them.

- Neither Clemenceau, Lloyd George nor Wilson were satisfied with the outcome of the treaties; people in Britain and France felt that the treaties should have been harsher, while the people of the USA felt they were too harsh.

- People in some of the defeated countries hated and felt humiliated by the treaties – there were revolts in Germany and Turkey.

SUMMARY

- Many were left unsatisfied with the treaties, including the Big Three: Clemenceau felt the Treaty of Versailles was not harsh enough, while Wilson and Lloyd George thought it was too harsh and would lead to war again in the future.

- People in Germany despised the Treaty of Versailles, in particular the war guilt clause and the reparations.

- Germany's wartime allies were also punished. The terms of the treaties were so harsh that they led to economic collapse in Austria and Hungary, and a revolution in Turkey.

- Historians writing throughout the twentieth century have said that treaties were too harsh, crippling the countries they affected and leaving them bankrupt, divided and vulnerable to attack.

- More recently, some historians have taken a different view, saying that that the peacemakers had a very hard job and that they did a good job considering the circumstances.

REVISION SKILLS

When you revise it is a good idea to mix up the topics you are revising. Try to learn the strengths and weaknesses of the treaties off by heart, and when you're confident you know them revise something else (like the actual terms of the Treaty of Versailles), then come back to the strengths and weaknesses.

 ## APPLY

WRITE AN ACCOUNT

a Make two flashcards that order the strengths and weaknesses of the treaties signed at the end of the First World War, according to how important you think they are.

b How did the redistribution of territory lead to problems after 1919?

 EXAMINER TIP

Revising the strengths and weaknesses of the treaties could help you if you are asked questions such as: why a cartoon opposes or supports the treaties; how useful two sources are for showing why people opposed or supported the treaties; or how far you agree with a statement about how successful the treaties were.

SOURCE ANALYSIS

 **SOURCE A** *A British cartoon from 1919, entitled 'A bitter pill to swallow'*

SOURCE B *A protest in Kiel, Germany, 1919*

▼ **SOURCE C** *Adapted from an article in a German newspaper printed on the day that the Treaty of Versailles was signed, 28 June 1919:*

> The disgraceful Treaty is being signed today. Don't forget it! We will never stop until we win back what we deserve.

a

 EXAM QUESTION **Source A** opposes the Treaty of Versailles. How do you know? Explain your answer using **Source A** and your own knowledge.

b

EXAM QUESTION How useful are **Sources B** and **C** to a historian studying the German reaction to the Treaty of Versailles?

 EXAMINER TIP

Start by breaking down the imagery in the cartoon. Who do the people represent, what are they doing, and what is used to show a negative opinion? Then link the cartoon to what you know about people's opinions about the treaty. Why did Germany find it 'hard to swallow'?

 EXAMINER TIP

Make sure you read the question carefully. It asks you about two sources, so it's important that you refer to both of them.

 **RECAP**

The formation of the League of Nations

The formation of the League of Nations was one of Wilson's Fourteen Points. The League's aims were to:

- get countries to collaborate to help to prevent war (**collective security**)

- encourage disarmament

- improve living and working conditions

- tackle deadly diseases.

The League was written into each of the treaties signed at the end of the war, to make people recognise and respect it. Initially 42 countries joined, but countries who lost the First World War, including Germany, were not allowed to join. Russia was not allowed to join because it was Communist. The USA refused to join.

Membership of the League did change over time, with Germany joining the League after agreeing the Locarno Treaty (1925). Russia was allowed to join in 1934, by which time there were 58 member states. Each state sent representatives to the **Assembly**, and had to agree unanimously on an issue before action was taken. Four

powerful countries were permanent members of the **Council**: Britain, France, Italy and Japan. However, although Britain supported the League, it felt that action would be limited. France thought the League could help keep it safe from German attack. The League set up the **Permanent Court of International Justice** in 1920, but it could only advise on arguments and could not forcefully back up verdicts. The League would deal with aggression through its **Covenant**, which included:

- mitigation

- moral condemnation

- economic sanctions

- military force.

REVISION SKILLS

A mnemonic could help you remember that the League would deal with issues using the **'four Ms'**: **M**itigation, **M**oral condemnation, **M**oney and **M**ilitary.

The League included many powerful countries, so these sanctions could be quite intimidating. However, the League did not have an army of its own to enforce its decisions; it relied on its members providing a force.

The structure of the League

The Assembly

An international parliament. Each member state sent a representative to meet once a year. They would vote on issues and decisions had to be unanimous.

The Council

Met more frequently than the Assembly. Four permanent members: Britain, France, Italy and Japan, plus four other countries that were elected to sit on the Council for three years. The Council could **veto** rulings made by the Assembly.

The Permanent Court of International Justice

An international court of law that could give hearings and advise the parties involved in an argument, but rulings were not compulsory so were easily ignored.

The Secretariat

In charge of administration and arranging any action that the League wanted to take.

Special Commissions

Special groups formed to tackle specific issues, such as the International Labour Organisation (ILO) and the Health Organisation.

 APPLY

HOW FAR DO YOU AGREE?

a Complete the table below to summarise what the strengths and weaknesses of the structure and organisation of the League were.

Strengths:	Weaknesses:

b **EXAM QUESTION** 'The structure of the League made it fair and strong.' How far do you agree?

EXAMINER TIP

Make sure you consider and explain both sides of the argument. When answering these types of questions in the exam you should try to use specific evidence to support your ideas. This activity will help you organise the evidence. You should try to link your ideas to specific events that the League was involved in.

SOURCE ANALYSIS

▶ **SOURCE A** *A cartoon entitled 'Muzzled?' published in the* London Opinion, *September 1919*

a Look at **Source A**. Describe what you can see.

b **EXAM QUESTION** Source A is critical of the League of Nations. How do you know? Explain your answer using **Source A** and your contextual knowledge.

Use the sentence starters and your answer to part **a** to answer the exam question:

I can tell that the source criticises the League because…

This suggests that…

Some people felt that the League would not be able to stop war because…

The work of the League's agencies

The League was not only set up to help prevent future conflict. It also used its special agencies and organisations to tackle social and economic issues.

International Labour Organisation (ILO)

 AIM: To improve working conditions

 In the 1920s, death rate of workers on Tanganyika railway reduced from over 50% to 4%

 In 1919, most members refused to stop children under the age of 14 from working as it would be too expensive

Commission for Refugees

 AIM: To help people who had lost their homes because of war, by improving refugee camps, helping them to return home, or finding new homes

 Helped free around 427,000 of the 500,000 prisoners of war still imprisoned after the First World War

 During the 1930s, failed to help Jews trying to flee Nazi Germany

Slavery Commission

 AIM: To end slavery

 During the 1920s, the League set free 200,000 slaves from Sierra Leonne

Economic and Financial Committee

 AIM: To improve living conditions

 Sent financial advisers to Austria and Hungary to rebuild their economies when they went bankrupt in 1921

 Unable to cope with global depression after 1929

Organisation for Communications and Transport

 AIM: To improve how countries worked together

 Introduced shipping lanes and an international highway code

Health Organisation

 AIM: To cure diseases

 Sent doctors to help in Turkish refugee camps

Permanent Central Opium Board (became Permanent Central Narcotics Board after 1925)

 AIM: To tackle the trade of illegal drugs

 Blacklisted four large companies involved in trading drugs illegally

 Some countries in the League did not want to stop the trade of opium as they made so much money from it

 APPLY

REVISION SKILLS

Keep your revision realistic – you are unlikely to remember every piece of information! Think carefully about the type of questions you might be asked for each topic and ensure you can recall enough evidence when answering these sort of questions. Creating flashcards, similar to those on these pages, is a good way of doing this.

WRITE AN ACCOUNT

Come up with your own acronym or mnemonic to help you remember the different agencies of the League.

EXAMINER TIP

For 'Write an account' exam questions you should include facts and figures to make points stand out and be memorable.

REVISION SKILLS

For longer questions always plan your answer. Aim to write three paragraphs and a conclusion. Jot down a few points to give a shape to your answer, and practise planning answers to questions.

HOW FAR DO YOU AGREE?

 **EXAM QUESTION** 'The League of Nations was successful in achieving its aims of improving working conditions and curing diseases.' How far do you agree with this statement? Explain your answer.

Plan your answer to the exam question above by completing the table below:

	Improving working conditions:	Healthcare and curing diseases:
Successes:		
Failures:		

REVIEW

Refer back to pages 26–28 to remind youself of what the League's aims were.

EXAMINER TIP

In the 'How far do you agree?' exam questions you need to explain two sides of the issue and sustain an overall judgment throughout your answer. Plan your overall judgment – try to think of a 'twist' to your answer, such as considering whether these aims were successfully achieved in the short or long term, or whether the set-up of the League meant that it was always doomed to fail.

The contribution of the League to peace in the 1920s

Many problems remained in Europe after the First World War. Europe had changed considerably, and the League had many disputes to solve during the 1920s. How successful was it in solving these?

Success: Åaland Islands, 1921

Sweden and Finland both claimed the Åaland Islands. The League gave the islands to Finland, but forbid the building of forts on them. Both countries accepted the decision.

Failure and success: Upper Silesia, 1921–25

A **plebiscite** was held to decide whether Upper Silesia, which was on the Germany–Poland border, should be German or Polish. Germany won 60% of the vote, but Poland claimed this had been fixed. The League split Upper Silesia into areas according to how they had voted; Germany complained that Poland got most of the industrial areas and Poland complained that they had around half the population, but only one third of the land. However, both countries did (grudgingly) accept the League's decision, which could be seen as a success.

Failure: Corfu, 1923

An Italian general and his team were murdered while surveying land in Greece. Mussolini demanded compensation and for the murderers to be executed, but Greece did not know who the murderers were so could not do this. Mussolini invaded Corfu. The League condemned Mussolini, but he undermined them by complaining to the Conference of Ambassadors. Greece was forced to apologise to Mussolini and to pay compensation. Mussolini had shown that the League could not enforce justice when one country involved was a larger, stronger country. The League could be ignored or bullied by strong countries.

Failure: Vilna, 1920–21

Vilna was the capital of Lithuania, a new country, but there were many Polish people living there. The Polish army invaded and Lithuania asked the League for help, but the League did nothing as Poland was a strong ally against Germany.

Failure and success: Bulgaria, 1925

Greece invaded Bulgaria when Greek soldiers were killed on the border. The League forced Greece to withdraw and pay compensation. However, this seemed hypocritical since the League had allowed Mussolini, a much more powerful leader, to get away with something very similar in Corfu.

Map labels: FINLAND, SWEDEN, Åaland Islands, LITHUANIA, VILNA, BELARUS, UNITED KINGDOM, GERMAN REICH (WEIMAR REPUBLIC), POLAND, Upper Silesia, FRANCE, AUSTRIA, ITALY, BULGARIA, ALBANIA, GREECE

SUMMARY

- The League of Nations was founded to keep world peace through collective security.

- There were problems with how the League was organised, such as the need for a unanimous vote and the fact that countries like Britain and France had too much power.

- During the 1920s, the League was successful in dealing with humanitarian issues, such as refugees, and when negotiating with small countries.

- However, if a strong country like Italy wanted to ignore the League, they could, and Britain and France could undermine the League if it suited them.

⚙ APPLY

WRITE AN ACCOUNT

a In what ways can the League be seen to have been successful in the 1920s?
The League could be seen as successful in Upper Silesia because …

_____

_____

The League could be seen as successful in the Åaland Islands because …

_____

_____

The League could be seen as successful in Bulgaria because …

_____

_____

b In what ways can the League be seen to have failed in the 1920s?
The League could be seen to have failed in Vilna because …

_____

_____

The League could be seen to have failed in Upper Silesia because …

_____

_____

The League could be seen to have failed in Corfu because …

_____

_____

The League could be seen to have failed in Bulgaria because …

_____

_____

c **EXAM QUESTION** Write an account of how the League of Nations failed to keep peace in Europe throughout the 1920s.

HOW FAR DO YOU AGREE?

You might be asked whether you agree that the League was successful (or not) during the 1920s. Create a flashcard to help you plan how you would answer this type of question.

EXAMINER TIP

Make sure you explain how and why the League failed in each event. The examiner wants to know not only what happened, but also why the League was unable to resolve things. You have practised this skill in parts **a** and **b**. Try to structure your answer in chronological order.

REVIEW

The effects of the Great Depression are another reason for the failure of the League in the 1930s. Look ahead to Chapter 6 to remind yourself of how this global event had an impact on the work of the League of Nations.

CHAPTER 5

Diplomacy outside the League

RECAP

International agreements

Certain countries made a number of agreements between themselves during the 1920s, including countries that were not members of the League, such as the USA. It is possible that these nations were simply trying to find as many different ways as possible to secure peace – or, perhaps, that they had little faith in the League's ability to uphold it.

Locarno Treaties

Who? France and Germany, represented by their **foreign ministers** Briand and Stresemann

When? 1925

Where? Locarno, Switzerland

What?

- The two enemies agreed to work together peacefully.

- Germany accepted the terms of the Treaty of Versailles.

- Other countries like Britain and Italy also signed and each country agreed not to go to war with each other; if one country broke the treaties the others would support the country that was invaded.

Why wasn't the League involved?

- Germany suggested the treaties and it was not part of the League.

Why were the treaties significant?

- It seemed as if Germany was accepting the Treaty of Versailles, especially the terms about territory, and trying to become a peaceful nation.

- Relationships between countries, especially France and Germany, improved – this paved the way to Germany being allowed to join the League of Nations.

- The League should have been leading the way on such an important agreement, especially since it involved two of the League's powerful members; Britain and France.

Kellogg-Briand Pact

Who? 65 countries, including Germany, France and the USA

When? 1928

Where? Paris, France

What?

- The countries agreed war would not be used to solve disputes between them.

Why wasn't the League involved?

- Germany and the USA were not members.

Why was the treaty significant?

- The fact that the League was not involved made it look like it was a place to talk, not for actual solutions, and this damaged its reputation.

Other agreements

Washington Arms Conference (or the Washington Naval Conference), 1921–22

- Major countries like Britain, the USA, Japan and France agreed the maximum size of their navies.

- The League was not the one pushing for disarmament, and countries like Britain and France attended independently of the League.

Rapallo Treaty, 1922

- Germany and Russia agreed to work together.

- The League was not involved as Germany and Russia were not members.

SUMMARY

- The League of Nations should have been at the forefront of any international agreements that encouraged peace or disarmament. However, during the 1920s many international agreements were signed without the League, which damaged its reputation.

- While the USA, Russia and Germany were not in the League it meant that it could not be at the forefront of international politics, so its success would be limited. Russia and Germany did eventually join, but left in the 1930s.

 APPLY

SOURCE ANALYSIS

▼ **SOURCE A** *Adapted from a speech given by Fridjhof Nansen at the Nobel Peace Prize ceremony in 1926; Nansen had won the prize in 1922 for his work helping refugees and was presenting the prize to Briand and Stresemann for creating the Locarno Treaties:*

> The Locarno agreements mark a radical and complete change in European politics, transforming the relations between the former antagonists in the war and infusing them with an entirely new spirit. This spirit derives from the almost previously unknown attempt to base politics on the principle of mutual friendship and trust.

▼ **SOURCE B** *A picture of the signing of the Kellogg-Briand Pact from a French magazine published in August 1928*

a   Look at **Sources A** and **B** and highlight or write down anything that tells you what the Locarno Treaties and the Kellogg-Briand Pact achieved.

b   Why was it important that the League was not involved in these treaties?

c   Use your answers to parts **a** and **b** to answer the exam question below.

> **EXAM QUESTION** Study **Source A** and **B**. How useful are **Sources A** and **B** to a historian studying the League of Nations? Explain your answer using **Sources A** and **B** and your contextual knowledge.

 EXAMINER TIP

First, use the content of each source, linked to your own knowledge, to explain what it tells us about the League of Nations. Then use the provenance – think about **TAPAS**: **T**ime, **A**uthor, **P**urpose, **A**udience, **S**ite (where was the source created?) to work out how useful the sources are. You should presume that the sources are useful – don't write about things that the sources don't tell you about the League: no source can tell you everything!

CHAPTER 6

The collapse of the League

RECAP

The League of Nations had some successes in the 1920s. However, in the 1930s it failed to perform its main role as a peacekeeping force. In particular, the League failed to act against the aggressiveness of Japan, Italy and Germany.

The Manchurian crisis

Causes

- In 1929, the **Wall Street Crash** started the **Great Depression**. Japan suffered greatly; its main export was silk, a luxury item that most people could not afford during the Depression.
- Japan became more militaristic – the government looked for land to invade, thinking it would give them more natural resources. Manchuria, in north China, was rich in natural resources.
- Japan already had industry and a railway there so it looked like an ideal place to invade.

Key

▨ Japanese expansion

········· South Manchurian railway

Events

18 September 1931: The **Mukden Incident**. An explosion occurred on the Japanese-owned South Manchurian Railway. Japan blamed China but the Chinese denied that they were involved.

February 1932: The Japanese government had wanted friendship with Manchuria but the army ignored this and invaded it. When the people reacted positively the government decided not to stop the army's invasion. Soon a 'puppet leader' (one Japan could control) was put in charge of Manchuria.

March 1932: China appealed to the League, which was reluctant to act: Japan was one of its leading members and Manchuria was far from Europe, where the League was based. The League did, however, issue a moral condemnation.

Japan ignored the League. There was very little the League could do without its own army, and its members didn't want to send their own armies so far away. Economic sanctions would be useless as Japan's main trade partner, the USA, was not part of the League.

April 1932: The League sent British politician Lord Lytton to investigate; he took nearly a year to write his report (published in October 1932), by which time Japan had invaded Manchuria. Lytton concluded that Japan was in the wrong, but Japan ignored the report, left the League, and went on to occupy more Chinese territory from 1933 to 1937.

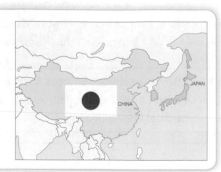

Consequences:

- One of the League's own members had ignored its moral condemnation and instructions to withdraw.

- Without an army of its own the League was powerless.

- However, most people continued to have faith in the League – they thought that if a similar event happened in Europe then the League would be able to deal with it.

- Other militaristic countries like Italy and Germany saw how powerless the League of Nations really was.

The Lytton Report took far too long; by the time it was finished, Japan was in control of Manchuria

Asia was far away and not viewed as vital to the countries in Europe; as a result, they did not want to commit resources to dealing with the issues there

Why did the League fail?

The Depression was already damaging world trade and League members were unwilling to impose economic sanctions

Countries were unwilling to take military action because it would be expensive and unpopular with the public

 APPLY

WRITE AN ACCOUNT

a Explain how each of the following factors led to the League's failure to resolve the Manchurian crisis:

Great Depression	
League did not have its own army	
Membership of the League	
Japan undermining the League	

b Write an account of how events in Manchuria led to an international crisis between 1931 and 1933.

Look at the exam question above. Plan your answer by writing four or five headings that summarise what happened. These should be in chronological order and will form the paragraphs of your answer. Then, use your answers to part **a** to make notes on the detail that each paragraph will cover.

REVIEW

In order to give a more detailed explanation of how the Depression led to the downfall of the League in areas other than the Manchurian crisis, look ahead to pages 38–39.

HOW FAR DO YOU AGREE?

 'The main consequence of the Manchurian crisis was that the League's reputation remained intact.' How far do you agree with this statement? Explain your answer.

EXAMINER TIP

You need to explain the causes and consequences of these events, showing how each step led to an increase in tension. Start with the effect the Depression had on Japan and how this led to the decision to invade Manchuria. Then, move on to explaining the Mukden Incident and the League's reaction. Finally, think about Japan's reaction to the League, and how the League was powerless to stop Japan's invasion of China. If you can demonstrate how each of these factors led to the next, you will be more likely to achieve Level 4.

The Abyssinian crisis

While the crisis in Manchuria continued, the League had to deal with invasion of the African nation of Abyssinia in 1935.

Causes

Mussolini wanted to invade Abyssinia in Africa for a number of reasons:

- He wanted to rebuild the Roman Empire, by invading other countries.

- There were lots of natural resources in Abyssinia, which would be useful for Italy during the Depression.

- In 1896, Italy had tried to invade Abyssinia and was humiliated when this poor country defeated them — Mussolini wanted revenge.

- He was confident that the League would not stop him as they had backed down to him before, during the Corfu crisis in 1923.

- In 1935, Britain and France signed an agreement with Italy to form the **Stresa Front**. Mussolini did not think Britain or France would endanger the new agreement by trying to stop him in Abyssinia.

REVIEW

To refresh your knowledge of the Corfu crisis see page 30.

Events

December 1934: Italian troops clashed with Abyssinians at Wal Wal. The League failed to stop Mussolini, who was intent on war.

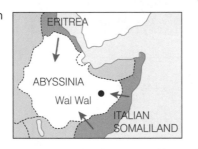

January 1935: The French foreign minister, Pierre Laval, made a secret agreement with Italy: Mussolini could deal with Abyssinia however he wanted and France would not interfere.

October 1935: Italian troops entered Abyssinia. The League condemned the invasion, but Mussolini ignored them and even used chemical weapons.

30 June 1935: The Abyssinian emperor, **Haile Selassie**, addressed the League, but still the League did nothing.

5 May 1936: Italian troops entered the capital, Addis Ababa.

May 1936: Italy left the League of Nations.

Why did the League fail?

Britain and France didn't close the Suez Canal (which would have made it difficult for Mussolini to get troops to Abyssinia) because they didn't want to upset Mussolini.

When the League imposed trade sanctions on Italy it failed to ban steel, oil and coal as it felt this would damage their member's economies. These were resources that Mussolini needed for the invasion.

The League banned sales of arms to Abyssinia, which left them defenceless.

The **Hoare-Laval Pact** was a secret agreement suggested by the British and French foreign ministers. They wanted to give Mussolini land in Abyssinia. The pact was leaked by the press and there was public outcry; leading members had proven they were willing to undermine the League for their own self-interest.

Consequences for the League

- Britain and France showed that they cared more about their own interests.

- Small countries knew the League could and would do nothing to protect them. From this time onwards, almost no one regarded the League as a serious or powerful organisation.

 **APPLY**

HOW FAR DO YOU AGREE?

a   Make a series of flashcards that help you to memorise the causes, events and consequences of the Abyssinian crisis.

b   'The Abyssinian crisis was the main reason the League of Nations failed.' How far do you agree with this statement? Plan an answer for this question. Decide what evidence you would use for each side of the argument, and consider your overall judgment.

c   Use your plan for part **b** to write a full answer to the question.

SOURCE ANALYSIS

▶ **SOURCE A** *A British cartoon from 1935; the men on the left are Hoare and Laval*

a   What event is this source about? Write down three facts about this event.

b   Why did this event make the League look bad?

c   **EXAM QUESTION** **Source A** is critical of the League of Nations. How do you know? Explain your answer using **Source A** and your contextual knowledge.

REVISION SKILLS

Remember to be realistic when making flashcards. Don't include too much information. Bullet points, images and mnemonics/acronyms can all help you to remember things when you use your flashcards to self-test.

EXAMINER TIP

Be careful when explaining the factors that led to the collapse of the League — you need to think about how these weakened it. Use details of what happened to support your ideas, but don't simply describe what happened.

EXAMINER TIP

Remember to link your answer to your own knowledge. What do you know about these events that would support the cartoonist's view?

Did the Manchurian and Abyssinian crises lead to the collapse of the League?

Most historians agree that the League's inability to deal with the Manchurian and Abyssinian crises meant it was a failure, and that it had collapsed as a peace-keeping organisation. How can these two events be used as evidence of the League's failings?

Why did the League collapse?	Evidence from the Manchurian crisis	Evidence from the Abyssinian crisis
The Depression	Japan's main export was silk – a luxury item that people did not buy during the Depression, so the Japanese economy crashed Japan wanted to invade Manchuria because it was rich in natural resources The government in Japan was not popular – seizing land in Manchuria made the government appear strong and the victories against the Chinese took people's minds off the Depression	Mussolini came to power promising to rebuild the Roman Empire – invading Abyssinia was a distraction from what was going wrong in Italy Britain failed to inflict effective trade sanctions on Italy – they worried that banning the trade of coal would lead to further unemployment in Britain There were lots of natural resources in Abyssinia
The League was powerless without an army	When Japan ignored the League's warnings there was nothing the League could do	Mussolini used chemical weapons on the Abyssinians, who were left defenceless by the League
Economic sanctions did not work	Many members of the League felt that as the USA was Japan's main trade partner, economic sanctions would not have a major impact; therefore no sanctions were imposed on Japan	The League banned the sale of weapons to Abyssinia as well as Italy; this left their army with only basic weapons France and Britain failed to ban goods that Italy would need to invade, such as coal and oil
The League lacked important world powers such as the USA, the USSR and Germany	Many European powers felt that Manchuria was too far away to deal with As the USA was not a member of the League, Japan would not lose its main trade partner if the League imposed economic sanctions	Britain and France wanted to keep Mussolini on side as they saw him as an ally against Hitler

Britain and France dominated the League 	The dominating countries of the League were based in Europe and were reluctant to get involved in a matter so far away	Britain and France both had huge empires in Africa, so Mussolini felt they could not object to him taking colonies there too
	Britain sent Lord Lytton to investigate for the League, but he took too long – his report took many months to write by which time Japan had completed its invasion. As one of the dominating forces of the League, Britain had failed to act with enough speed, which made Japan's invasion easier	Britain and France failed to close the Suez Canal, which could have halted his invasion
		Mussolini was seen as an ally against Hitler, so Britain and France proposed the Hoare-Laval Pact which undermined the League

⚙ APPLY

WRITE AN ACCOUNT

Create a series of illustrated flashcards that shows the sequence of events of either the Manchurian or Abyssinian crisis.

EXAMINER TIP

You need to ensure you are familiar with the chronology and key events of each of these two crises, as you may be asked to write an account of them in an exam.

HOW FAR DO YOU AGREE?

In the exam, you could be asked about the main reason why the League failed. You will need to explain your answer. Practise doing this with the activity below.

a Write a PEE (Point, Evidence, Explanation) paragraph explaining how Britain and France's dominance in the League led to it failing. Use these sentence starters to help:

The League failed because Britain and France dominated it, and they put their self interests first. For example …

_____

_____

This meant that the League failed because...

_____

_____

b Now do the same, explaining why the Depression led to the collapse of the League, but this time without the sentence starters.

c Explain how the way the League was structured led to its collapse.

EXAMINER TIP

In the exam, students are often good at remembering the events of the Manchurian and Abyssinian crises and how the League reacted, but do not always develop their answers by explaining how and why these events demonstrate the failure of the League. Make sure you explain how these events made the League look weak, or undermined its authority.

The Depression and the rise of extremist parties

- In October 1929, the US economy crashed. The USA had lent money to many countries during the First World War and to help them rebuild after the war: therefore, when the USA went bust – so did everyone else.

- The Depression brought with it vast unemployment, homelessness and starvation on a global scale. In these desperate times people started to lose confidence in their governments and to demand change.

- Many were won over by the promises of dictators such as Hitler, who came to power in 1933. He had vowed to make Germany great again by invading other countries, which he promised would end the Depression by providing employment in weapons factories and the army.

- In Japan, the army took over the country; Stalin controlled the USSR; and in Italy Mussolini was dictator.

REVIEW

There is more specific detail about Hitler's promises and how they led to war on page 42.

The failure of the League to avert war in 1939

- People turned to extremism and militarism in the hope of rebuilding their countries' economies, and this meant that these countries were less likely to support the League's aims of cooperation and peace. For example, Hitler stormed out of the League's disarmament conference in 1933.

- Hitler and Mussolini promised glory for their countries by waging war. They were not afraid of the League's moral condemnation, and governments could not impose trade sanctions as their economies were also weak due to the Depression, and they could not afford to lose deals.

- The only action Hitler and Mussolini could not have ignored was sending in an army, but of course the League did not have armed forces of its own and other countries could not afford to lend theirs in this time of Depression.

- In this climate, war became more and more likely and the League was powerless to stop it.

SUMMARY

- The Manchurian crisis made the League look inefficient and ineffective.

- Britain and France undermined the League during the Abyssinian crisis. By the end of the crisis no one really respected the League.

- The Depression meant that the League faced dictators who were determined to start wars. The League had always been fragile, but against determined aggressors like Hitler and Mussolini it stood no chance.

 **APPLY**

HOW FAR DO YOU AGREE?

 EXAM QUESTION 'The main reason the League of Nations failed was the Depression.' How for do you agree with this statement? Explain your answer.

a The table below gives reasons for the League's failure. Add **evidence** from your own knowledge by writing in an event that proves that each reason led to failure.

Point:		Evidence:	Explanation:
Depression			

Ineffective trade sanctions			
Absence of powerful countries such as the USA			
Slow and inefficient decision-making	??		
Self-interest of dominant members such as Britain and France			
Manchurian crisis			
Abyssinian crisis			

b Next, **explain** why each reason led to the failure of the League. Think about the impact: how did it affect the League's reputation, prove that it could not achieve its aims, or convince others that they could threaten war without the League taking action?

c Use your ideas from parts **a** and **b** to have a go at the exam question. Remember, you don't have to explain every factor. Explain the one from the question, but then aim to explain two others.

EXAMINER TIP

In order to achieve Level 2 or higher in this type of question, you need to explain your ideas. Writing in PEE paragraphs will help:

- First make your **point**. What reason for the League's failure will you look at in the paragraph? You should examine the reason mentioned in the question as well as other possible reasons.

- Next, illustrate your answer with **evidence**. Make sure your evidence is specific and relevant. Giving details like dates, names, places and statistics can help.

- Finally, **explain**. Link your evidence back to the question. You might want to come up with a 'magic sentence' to use at the end of every paragraph to keep your ideas focused on the question. In this answer your magic sentence could be 'this meant the League failed because …'.

REVISION SKILLS

Try using a memory aid like a mnemonic or an acronym to help you remember the reasons for the League's failure. Look at the factors given on the table – how could you remember these?

CHAPTER 7

The development of tension

 **RECAP**

Hitler's aims

Hitler became chancellor of Germany in 1933. His foreign policy aims are summarised below:

- *L*ebensraum

- *O*verturn Versailles

- *U*nite German speaking people (*Volksdeutsche*) in a Greater Germany (this included *Anschluss*)

- *De*stroy Communism

- *R*earmament

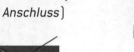

 REVISION SKILLS

Saying that Hitler's demands grew 'LOUDeR' might help you to remember his aims in the exam.

 REVIEW

You can remind yourself what these terms mean by looking back to page 14.

 REVIEW

The impact of the Depression is explored in more detail on page 40.

The reaction of Britain and France

Britain and France did not want to start another war, so they let Hitler get away with breaking the Treaty of Versailles, even though it was international law. They did this because:

- they needed time to rearm; their armies were not big enough to fight and win a war
- many people in Britain thought that Hitler was being reasonable because the Treaty of Versailles had been too harsh
- they were concerned about the USSR and thought that Hitler could be a valuable ally against Communism
- countries could not afford to go to war during the Depression and their governments were preoccupied with problems at home
- people could remember the horrors of the First World War: they did not want another war
- the policy followed by Britain and France from 1937 is known as appeasement: they tried to give Hitler what he wanted in the hope of preventing a war.

The reaction of the USSR and the USA

Joseph Stalin, the leader of the USSR, was worried by Hitler's determination to destroy Communism and by 1935 he was willing to put aside concerns about Britain and France in order to sign a mutual assistance treaty with France. Stalin would work with the allies to protect the USSR from Hitler.

The USA followed a policy of isolationism during the Depression. In 1934, a poll said that 70% of Americans did not want to get involved if a second war in Europe broke out.

⚙ **APPLY**

SOURCE ANALYSIS

▼ **SOURCE A** Adapted from *Mein Kampf*, written by Adolf Hitler, 1925:

> What a use could be made of the Treaty of Versailles! How each of its points could be branded into the hearts and minds of the German people until they find their souls aflame with rage and shame, and a will of steel is forged with the common cry, 'We will have arms again!'

 APPLY

SOURCE ANALYSIS

▼ **SOURCE B** *A British cartoon from 1938; the cartoon is called 'Nightmare waiting list'*

a Look at **Source B**. Find the following features:

   1 'All Germans everywhere are mine'

   2 'ghosts' holding signs that say 'Polish-Germans Crisis', 'Hungarian-Germans crisis' etc.

   3 a swastika – the Nazi flag

   4 'ghosts' with signs that read 'British Empire Germans Crisis' and 'USA Germans Crisis'

   5 Hitler.

b Why do you think the 'ghosts' representing the British and USA German Crises are positioned where they are?

c
> **EXAM QUESTION**
> Study **Source B**. **Source B** is critical of Hitler's foreign policy aims. How do you know? Explain your answer using **Source B** and your contextual knowledge.

d Look at **Source A**. Which of Hitler's foreign policy aims is **Source A** about?

e
> **EXAM QUESTION**
> Study **Sources A** and **B**. How useful are **Sources A** and **B** to a historian studying the causes of the Second World War?

The road to war

The Second World War broke out in early September 1939. Read through the following events leading up to the war and think about how each one raised tension and contributed to the war's outbreak.

Event	Reaction

1933: Hitler leaves the Disarmament Conference

The League of Nations held a conference encouraging all nations to disarm. When Hitler became chancellor he said he would disarm if everyone else did. If they didn't then he would disarm to the same level as France. When France refused Hitler stormed out of the conference and pulled Germany out of the League of Nations.

There was very little the allies could do. Hitler claimed that he had acted in a reasonable and fair way and that it was the French who were being unreasonable.

1934: The Dollfuss Affair

Fearful that Hitler would try to unite with Austria in *Anschluss,* the Austrian chancellor, Englebert Dollfuss, banned the Nazi Party in Austria. Hitler ordered Nazis to cause havoc in Austria and they murdered Dollfuss.

Mussolini moved his army to the Austrian border in support of Austria. Hitler was not ready to fight so he backed down.

13 January 1935: The Saar plebiscite

Under the Treaty of Versailles, the Saar had been controlled by the League of Nations for 15 years. In 1935, a plebiscite took place to decide whether Germany or France should control the area. 90% voted for Germany and Hitler used this as propaganda.

Hitler gained valuable resources, like the coalfields of the Saar, and there was nothing anyone could do as the plebiscite was fair and legal.

March 1935: Rearmament

Hitler held a rally where he announced that he had been rebuilding the German army and was reintroducing conscription. He had also started to develop the Luftwaffe – an air force.

In April 1935 Britain, France and Italy agreed that they would work together against Hitler as the Stresa Front.

June 1935: Anglo-German Naval Agreement

Britain signed an agreement allowing Germany to have a navy that was 35% of the size of the British navy.

Hitler realised that Britain was allowing him to break the terms of the Treaty of Versailles.

SUMMARY

- Hitler's foreign policy aims meant he needed to invade other countries; to do this he would need to build an army and to break the terms of the Treaty of Versailles.

- Other countries were reluctant to intervene. Between 1933 and 1935 there was very little anyone could do to stop Hitler from taking actions that would lead to war.

 APPLY

HOW FAR DO YOU AGREE

a Which of Hitler's aims did he try to achieve in the following events? Copy the table below and complete the second row.

b Which of the terms of the Treaty of Versailles was Hitler trying to break in each event? Add these to the third row.

 EXAMINER TIP

There are other causes of the outbreak of the Second World War. Plan two paragraphs to explain how Hitler's foreign policy contributed to the outbreak of the Second World War. Add another paragraph to this answer after you have read pages 51–52 about appeasement.

	Dollfuss Affair	Saar plebiscite	Rearmament	Anglo-German Naval Agreement
Hitler's aim(s)				
Term(s) violated				

 EXAM QUESTION 'Hitler's foreign policy aims were the main cause of the outbreak of the Second World War.' How far do you agree with this statement?

SOURCE ANALYSIS

THE BOY WHO SHOULDN'T GROW UP.

JOHN BULL. "THERE'S YOUR NEW NAVY SUIT. NOW YOU MUST PROMISE ME YOU WON'T GROW OUT OF IT."
GERMANY. "WELL, AT ALL EVENTS I'LL PROMISE NOT TO UNLESS YOU GROW OUT OF YOURS."

◀ **SOURCE A** *A British cartoon from 1935; the sailor in the foreground is Britain, next to him is Germany, and France is sulking in the background*

a Label at least five features of **Source A**. Explain why the cartoonist has used this symbolism.

b **EXAM QUESTION** **Source A** criticises the Anglo-German Naval Agreement. How do you know?

 EXAMINER TIP

Always read the whole question carefully – it will give you clues about what to include. Here, it is important that you use evidence from the source but also your own knowledge about the event. Why did people criticise Britain for signing this agreement?

Escalation of tension

Why did Hitler remilitarise the Rhineland?

The Treaty of Versailles had forced Germany to demilitarise the area of the Rhineland on the border between Germany and France. Hitler wanted to take *Lebensraum* in east Europe, but to do this he would have to invade other countries. He knew France and Britain were likely to declare war if he did this, so he had to protect his western borders by **remilitarising** the Rhineland.

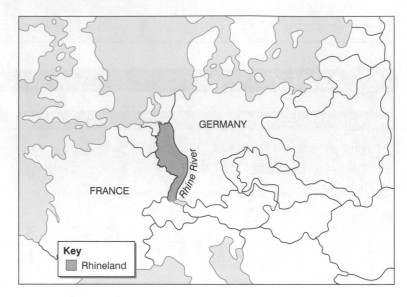

Hitler's big risk

German generals had advised Hitler that the army was not strong enough to fight if Britain or France chose to challenge it.

German financial ministers warned Hitler that if his plan failed he would have to pay huge fines, which Germany could not afford.

1935: The Franco-Soviet pact was signed – a deal between France and the USSR in which each agreed to assist the other if attacked; as a result, Hitler claimed he was under attack from France in the west and the USSR in the east.

→

7 March 1936: Hitler's troops entered the Rhineland, many rode on bicycles and there was no air support.

↓

Civilians in the Rhineland greeted the troops with flowers.

Why didn't anyone stop Hitler?

Britain	France
Depression causing problems at home meant Britain was reluctant to do anything	Politicians were distracted as they were fighting a general election
British people said there was no need to stop Hitler from 'marching into his own back garden'; many felt that Hitler had a right to defend his own borders and that this area was rightfully his	Much of the French army was in Tunisia in case they needed to intervene in the Abyssinian crisis
The British leadership was preoccupied with the Abyssinian crisis	Many believed that the German army entering the Rhineland was bigger than it was – they thought this was a battle they would not win

 REVIEW

For more details on the Abyssinian crisis look back to pages 36–37.

Britain and France started rearming; war was getting closer

The French priority was now protecting its own border; they started ignoring treaties they had signed to protect other countries

Hitler signed the Anti-Comintern Pact with Japan in November 1936; they agreed to work together against the threat of Communism; Italy later joined the alliance when it agreed to the Pact of Steel with Germany in 1939

Hitler gained confidence that he could get away with violating the Treaty of Versailles

Why was the remilitarisation of the Rhineland important?

Hitler showed that he was powerful; he signed the Rome-Berlin Axis with Mussolini

⚙️ APPLY

SOURCE ANALYSIS

◀ **SOURCE A** *A British cartoon from 1936, called 'The Goose Step'; this was the name for a type of march that Nazi troops used at parades; 'Pax Germanica' means 'German peace'*

a What evidence can you find in **Source A** that suggests that Hitler claimed he was acting in peace?

b What evidence can you find to show that the cartoonist does not agree that Hitler's actions were peaceful?

c

> **EXAM QUESTION** **Source A** criticises Hitler's remilitarisation of the Rhineland. How do you know? Explain your answer using **Source A** and your contextual knowledge.

WRITE AN ACCOUNT

> **EXAM QUESTION** Write an account of how Hitler's remilitarisation of the Rhineland contributed to international tension in 1936.

a Identify five key words that you might need to use when answering the exam question above.

b Now have a go at answering the question in full.

The road to war: *Anschluss*, 1938

Having remilitarised the Rhineland without opposition and secured his western borders, Hitler turned his attention to other countries, starting with Germany's old ally, Austria.

1
Germany had been ruled by Austria for 600 years, but in the Treaty of Versailles they were forbidden to unite.

2
Two of Hitler's foreign policy aims were to unite German-speaking people and to destroy the Treaty of Versailles.

3
In 1934, Hitler had Austrian Nazis murder Dollfuss, the Austrian chancellor, but backed down when Mussolini moved troops to the Austrian border.

4
In 1938, Austrian Nazis planned to get rid of the new chancellor, Schuschnigg, but police discovered and stopped this plot. Austrian Nazis were imprisoned, but Schuschnigg still felt vulnerable. He met with Hitler and agreed to give key positions in the Austrian government to Nazis in return for Hitler's support.

5
Hitler's puppet, Seyss-Inquart, was appointed as minister for the interior, with full power over the police in Austria. He now had full control of the Austrian police force, who turned a blind eye to Nazi terrorist attacks on the Austrian government.

6
Schuschnigg planned a plebiscite to prove that the people of Austria did not want to be ruled by Hitler, but Hitler demanded that this be delayed and then forced Schuschnigg to resign.

7
Hitler made Seyss-Inquart the new chancellor. Seyss-Inquart was a Nazi 'puppet' – Hitler controlled him. He claimed that Austria was in a state of chaos and asked Hitler to restore order, and so on 12 March Nazi forces entered Austria. Crowds of Austrians gathered in the streets to cheer the Nazi soldiers' arrival.

8
On 10 April the plebiscite was held, and the Nazis won 99% of the vote.

How did people react to *Anschluss*?

Austria

99% of people voted in favour of *Anschluss*, but polling stations were heavily policed by Nazi 'stormtroopers', and the 'yes' box on the ballot form was much larger than the 'no' one!

Britain

Some British people had decided that the Treaty of Versailles was too harsh on Germany, and since they thought that Germany and Austria were essentially the same country, they felt that Hitler should be allowed to unite the two.

France

Two days before Hitler's invasion the whole government had resigned. France was in no position to get involved.

Czechoslovakia

The Czech people feared that Hitler's policy of *Lebensraum* would mean that they would be invaded next. Britain and France agreed that they would protect Czechoslovakia if Hitler did invade.

Germany

Hitler was able to use *Anschluss* as a great propaganda victory. The German people were delighted to be uniting with their Austrian neighbours, and could see that Hitler was achieving his foreign policy aims of *Volksdeutsche* and creating a Greater Germany.

Anschluss meant that Hitler's next steps on the road to war were more easily achieved: he could now use the Austrian army; he could access the east much more easily through Austria; and the Sudetenland of Czechoslovakia was now bordered by Germany (and Austria) on three sides.

APPLY

WRITE AN ACCOUNT

a Create a timeline that summarises the events between 1934 and 1938 that led to *Anschluss*.

b Why was each event important? Think about the impact it had on Hitler and other countries when you explain your answer.

c

> EXAM QUESTION Write an account of how Hitler's attempts to unite Germany with Austria contributed to international tension between 1934 and 1938.

REVIEW

To remind yourself of other events leading to *Anschluss*, such as the Dollfuss Affair, look back to Chapter 7.

EXAMINER TIP

Lots of students lose marks because they simply describe what happened, rather than explaining their ideas. This activity will help you to develop the skill of explaining the importance of events, which will help you in the 'write an account' exam question.

EXAMINER TIP

Look carefully at any dates in an exam question — they'll tell you what to include, so when you revise make sure you learn the dates of key events.

The Sudeten Crisis, 1938

Hitler had taken many steps on the road to war and was getting more and more confident that he could do as he pleased without anyone trying to stop him. None of his actions had been violent, but his next step was to change this.

A map showing the Sudetenland

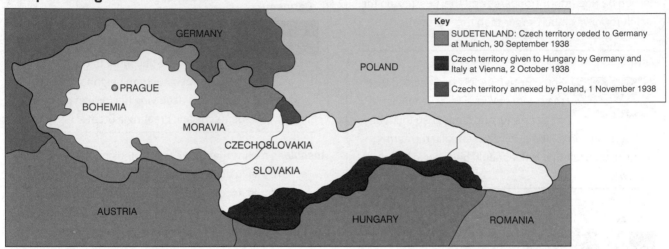

The Sudetenland was part of Czechoslovakia, on the German border.

Hitler planned to take *Lebensraum*.

Czechoslovakia's main defences were in the Sudetenland, so taking it would allow Hitler to invade the whole country. There were natural resources and factories in the area that Hitler could utilise in his war effort.

Czechoslovakia had been created at the end of the First World War. Hitler felt that the invasion of Czechoslovakia would be another step towards destroying the Treaty of Versailles.

About 20% of the Sudeten population was German. In May 1938, Hitler claimed they were being persecuted and used this as an excuse to attack.

Chamberlain meets Hitler, 15 September 1938

- Chamberlain flew to Berchtesgarden to meet Hitler.
- Chamberlain wanted to **appease** Hitler to prevent war, so agreed to allow Hitler to take the Sudetenland so long as his actions were peaceful.
- Chamberlain then met with the Czechs and forced them to agree to Hitler's terms.
- On 22 September, Chamberlain met Hitler at Bad Godsberg, where Hitler changed his demands: the Sudetenland would be handed over to him by 1 October and Hungary and Poland must also be given Czech land.

The Munich Conference, 29 September 1938

- Chamberlain, Hitler, Mussolini and Daladier (the French president) met in Munich.
- They accepted the demands Hitler had made at Bad Godsberg.
- Chamberlain and Daladier said they had prevented war, as Hitler promised not to take any more land. Chamberlain said he had guaranteed 'peace in our time'.
- The Czechs were not consulted.
- The USSR was not consulted. This made Stalin think that he could not trust Britain and France.

Hitler invades the Sudetenland, 10 October 1938

Troops marched in, but unlike events in the Rhineland and Austria, the Czechs saw this as a real military invasion.

This was first time Hitler had invaded a country that had never previously been united with Germany.

Hitler completed his invasion of Czechoslovakia in 1939. He had broken the promises he had made at the Munich Conference and Chamberlain had to accept that his policy of appeasement had failed.

 APPLY

SOURCE ANALYSIS

◀ **SOURCE A** *A Russian cartoon from 1938; the caption reads 'Onwards to the east!' and the 'meat' on the plate is labelled Czechoslovakia*

▼ **SOURCE B** *Adapted from a note from General Ismay, the Secretary of the Committee of Imperial Defence, to the British Cabinet, sent on 20 September 1938:*

If Germany swallows up Czechoslovakia it will enhance German military prestige, increase German potential for war, and enable Germany to deploy stronger land forces against France and ourselves than can be done at present.

a Look at **Source A**. There are four characters in the cartoon, representing Britain, France, the USA and Germany. Label the cartoon to show which figure represents each country and write a short sentence to explain why they appear as they do.

b Read through **Source B**, and highlight every reason given for Hitler's wanting the Sudetenland.

c **EXAM QUESTION** Study **Sources A** and **B**. How useful are **Sources A** and **B** to a historian studying the reasons Hitler invaded Czechoslovakia?

EXAMINER TIP

Remember that the examiner is looking for positive evaluation – the sources will be useful. Work out how each source links to what you know about events, and make sure that you deal with both sources.

The ending of appeasement

Hitler had grown confident that no one would stop him from taking over wherever he wanted. However, when he invaded Czechoslovakia other countries finally realised that appeasing him was not working. Many historians have argued that the policy of appeasement was a big mistake.

Arguments for and against appeasement

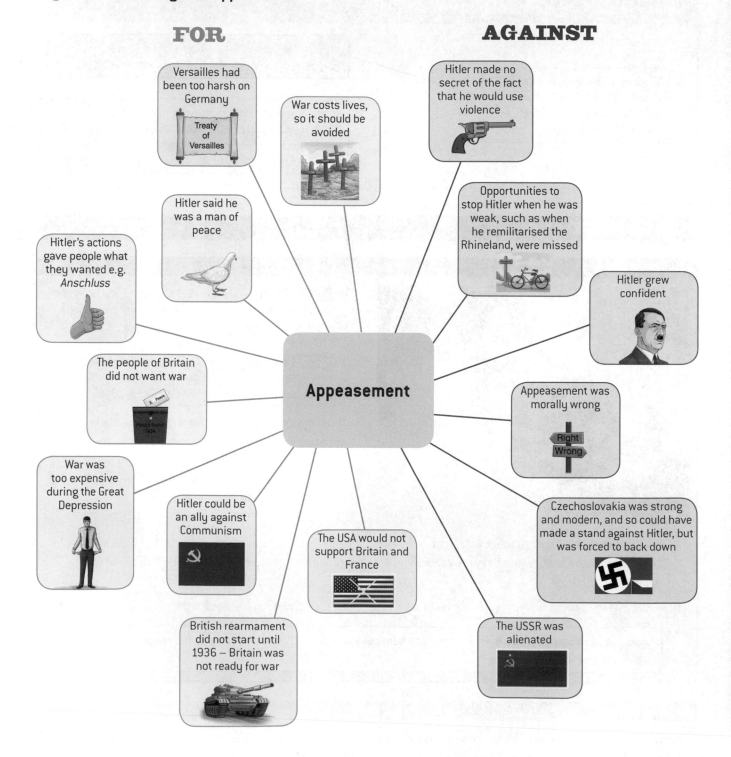

SUMMARY

- Hitler's foreign policy meant he would invade other countries.

- However, Britain and France were reluctant to go to war, so followed the policy of appeasement.

- This taught Hitler he could do as he wanted and so Europe got closer to war, as he remilitarised the Rhineland, forced *Anschluss* on Austria, invaded the Sudetenland, and then took the rest of Czechoslovakia.

APPLY

SOURCE ANALYSIS

▼ **SOURCE A** *A British cartoon from 3 October 1938; Chamberlain is facing Mars, the Roman god of war*

a Look at **Source A**. Why do you think Chamberlain is drawn with a hat and an umbrella?

b **EXAM QUESTION** **Source A supports the policy of appeasement. How do you know?** Explain your answer using **Source A** and your contextual knowledge.

HOW FAR DO YOU AGREE?

Make two flashcards summarising the arguments for and against appeasement.

REVISION SKILLS

Making revision flashcards is a good way of revising and creating a useful revision aid for later use. Jot down three or four things under a heading on each card. Try to include a factual detail with each point.

CHAPTER 9

The outbreak of war

The Nazi-Soviet Pact

Hitler's next victim would be Poland – here he could take more *Lebensraum*, as well as continue to defy the terms of the Treaty of Versailles by invading land that was taken away from Germany in 1919. However, the USSR considered Poland to be part of its sphere of influence, so invading meant Hitler could face a war on two fronts – Britain and France in the west and the USSR in the east – which was one of the reasons Germany lost the First World War. Hitler had to eliminate the threat of the USSR, so on 23 August 1939 Hitler and Stalin signed the Nazi-Soviet Pact.

What was in it for Germany?

- Hitler could invade Poland without facing a war on two fronts. Britain and France had promised to protect Poland, but the USSR would not interfere.
- Britain and France would now face war with Germany without the USSR as their ally.
- The USSR had a massive army, which would no longer be a threat to Germany.

What was in it for the USSR?

- Stalin felt Britain and France had snubbed him by leaving him out of the Munich Conference and he thought they were being weak by appeasing Hitler. He realised he could not trust them to help protect the USSR if Hitler invaded.
- Britain and France had sent minor diplomats with no real authority to meet with Stalin. Hitler had sent a senior Nazi; he seemed to respect the USSR.
- Hitler agreed that Stalin would be given Polish territory. Stalin would not even have to send troops.
- Stalin feared that Hitler would invade the USSR, but he was not ready to fight. Becoming allies bought him time to prepare.
- Land in Poland would act as a buffer zone if Hitler did decide to invade the USSR.

 REVIEW

For more details on the Munich Conference revisit pages 50–51.

The invasion of Poland and the declaration of war

The Nazi-Soviet Pact meant that Britain and France realised that the policy of appeasement had failed. They had already agreed to protect Poland if Hitler invaded, and now they formalised this agreement; war seemed inevitable. Without the threat of war on two fronts, Hitler felt confident enough to invade Poland. On 1 September 1939, a German battleship attacked Danzig and the German army and Luftwaffe descended on Poland.

On 3 September 1939, the British sent an ultimatum – Hitler must leave Poland by 11.00am or Britain would declare war. Hitler sent no reply, so Britain, followed by France, declared war.

Poland was overrun within four weeks, and Hitler thought Britain and France would back down. He was wrong.

APPLY

HOW FAR DO YOU AGREE?

a Make a timeline of the events that led to war between 1933 (disarmament conference) and September 1939.

b On your timeline, colour code events that could be used as evidence that the following factors led to war: Hitler's foreign policy; the Treaty of Versailles; the Depression; appeasement; the Nazi-Soviet Pact.

c EXAM QUESTION
'The signing of the Nazi-Soviet Pact was the main reason for the outbreak of the Second World War.' How far do you agree with this statement? Explain your answer.

EXAMINER TIP

To be awarded the top level mark, you need to have a sustained judgement running all the way through your answer. To do this you will need to plan ahead. You might want to think about how the Nazi-Soviet Pact was the short-term cause, but that it wouldn't have been signed without other, long-term, causes. Can you explain a link between causes?

SOURCE ANALYSIS

▼ **SOURCE A** *'Strange Bedfellows' by British cartoonist, Bert Thomas; published in a British newspaper, 18 September 1939*

 EXAM QUESTION
Sources A opposes the Nazi-Soviet Pact. How do you know? Explain your answer by using **Source A** and your contextual knowledge.

REVIEW

You will need to look back at Chapters 7, 8 and 9 in order to make a complete timeline of the road to war.

REVISION SKILLS

We remember information better when it is colourful or has images with it. Try adding pictures to your timeline to act as memory prompts. Use sketches, doodles, and pictures to help make your facts memorable. You do not have to be a good artist to do this!

EXAMINER TIP

Look carefully at the imagery used in the source. How does this show that the creator has a negative opinion? Once you've worked this out you need to link your ideas to what you know about the pact. Why did people question Hitler and Stalin's motives?

Who was responsible for the outbreak of the Second World War?

The Second World War broke out on 3 September 1939, when Hitler ignored demands from Britain and France that he withdraw from Poland. This was the short-term spark that ignited war. In reality the possibility of war had been building throughout the 1930s, and several people could be held responsible to some degree.

Hitler

- Wrote in his book *Mein Kampf* that he would use violence to make Germany strong again
- Foreign policy aims included *Lebensraum*, building a greater Germany, uniting German speaking people, and destroying the Treaty of Versailles, which meant he had to invade other countries
- Broke the Treaty of Versailles, which was international law
- Invaded Poland, which prompted Britain and France to declare war

Chamberlain

- Missed opportunities to stop Hitler, because of appeasement
- Failed to act when Hitler remilitarised the Rhineland. At this stage the Nazis were not ready for war – if Chamberlain had acted Hitler would have been forced to stop
- Gave the Sudetenland to Hitler without consulting the Czechs, then allowed Hitler to invade a country he had no claim to, which enabled him to strengthen his army
- Excluded Stalin from the Munich Conference, which alienated Stalin and prompted him to sign the Nazi-Soviet Pact

Stalin

- Signed the Nazi-Soviet Pact despite Hitler wanting to destroy Communism
- The size of the USSR's armed forces meant Hitler had a huge and powerful ally
- The pact meant Hitler would not have to fight a war on two fronts, so he was able to invade Poland

Other factors

Japan

- Invaded Manchuria in 1931, walked out of the League of Nations in February 1933, and then mainland China in 1937 – which some historians say was the start of the Second World War
- Signed the Anti-Comintern Pact and Pact of Steel with Hitler

Mussolini

- Invaded Abyssinia which destroyed people's confidence in the League of Nations
- In 1938, did not intervene when Hitler carried out *Anschluss*, which convinced Hitler that he could do as he pleased
- Signed the Anti-Comintern Pact and the Pact of Steel with Hitler

The Big Three

- Treaty of Versailles was resented by Germany and inspired Hitler's foreign policy – to re-unite German speaking people, build a greater Germany and claim *Lebensraum*
- By the 1930s, many people felt that Versailles had been too harsh and turned a blind eye when Hitler started to break it

REVIEW

For more on the Abyssinian crisis see pages 36–37; for *Anschluss* see pages 48–49.

American isolationism

- This made the League weaker, so certain countries were prepared to act more aggressively and risk the outbreak of all-out war, because they didn't fear military action from the USA
- As a result of the USA's absence from the League, economic sanctions were useless because aggressive countries could trade with the USA

Fear of Communism

- Britain and France allowed Hitler to grow strong as they thought Germany could act as a buffer zone against Communism
- Their actions upset Stalin who agreed to the Nazi-Soviet Pact as he felt they would not support him if Hitler attacked

The Great Depression

- America demanded back loans from Germany as a result of the Depression; this led to the collapse of German industry and more people voting for Hitler, who was making many promises to them
- Some countries (such as Japan and Italy) acted more aggressively in order to secure supplies of raw materials and build empires

The weakness and collapse of the League of Nations

- Hitler saw that he could get away with invading other countries without being punished, just like Japan had done in Manchuria and Mussolini had in Abyssinia
- Major countries (such as the USA) were not members of the League, meaning it was not a forceful military or economic threat; the League did not have its own army

SUMMARY

- Hitler signed the Nazi-Soviet Pact, in spite of hating Communism, because it meant he could avoid a war on two fronts when he invaded Poland.
- Stalin signed it to gain territory and time to prepare for war with Hitler.
- Stalin knew Hitler would attack, but felt he could not rely on the USSR's old allies, Britain and France.
- The pact gave Hitler the confidence to attack Poland, but when he did Britain and France stood by their promise to protect Poland, and declared war. The Second World War started on 3 September 1939.

APPLY

WRITE AN ACCOUNT

a Write out the names of the different people and factors that could be held responsible for the start of the war. Each one should be written on a different piece of paper. Put these in order of who/what you feel was most responsible.

b Next, rearrange your cards into groups to show how factors link to each other. For example, how could you link the Treaty of Versailles to Chamberlain?

c **EXAM QUESTION** Write an account of how events in the 1930s led to the outbreak of the Second World War.

HOW FAR DO YOU AGREE?

 EXAM QUESTION 'Chamberlain was the individual who was most responsible for the outbreak of the Second World War.' How far do you agree with this statement? Explain your answer.

a Look at the list of other factors that led to the war outlined on these pages. Write a sentence explaining why each factor led to the outbreak of war.

b Have a go at the exam question above.

Exam practice

GCSE sample answers

⟳ REVIEW

On these exam practice pages, you will find a sample student answer for each of the exam questions for Paper 1: Section B: Conflict and Tension 1918—1939. What are the strengths and weaknesses of the answers? Read the following pages and think carefully about what the student has written, what the examiner has said about each answer, and how you might improve your own answers to the Conflict and Tension exam questions.

Source analysis questions

▼ **SOURCE A** *A British cartoon from 1921; David Lloyd George is talking to Aristide Braid, the French Foreign Minister; 'indemnity' refers to compensation that one country has to pay to another following a war*

" PERHAPS IT WOULD GEE-UP BETTER IF WE LET IT TOUCH EARTH "

 1 Study **Source A**. **Source A** opposes the Treaty of Versailles. How do you know? Explain your answer by using **Source A** and your contextual knowledge.

[4 marks]

Sample student answer

I know that the cartoon criticises the Treaty of Versailles because it shows David Lloyd George and Aristide Braid discussing the 'unlimited indemnity' that Germany, the horse, is facing. We can see that Germany is being weighed down because of the compensation it has to pay and this means that the horse is unable to move the cart forward. This is symbolic — Germany as a country cannot move forward because it is being weighed down by the terms of the treaty, so the cartoonist is clearly opposing this term of the treaty.

 REVISION SKILLS

You will always have two types of source questions in your Conflict and Tension exam. The first question (as here) deals with one source, the second question deals with two sources. Read page 8 for details on how to master your source analysis exam skills.

EXAMINER TIP

Here the student uses specific evidence from the source and explains what the symbolism means.

 EXAMINER TIP

 It is always a good idea to refer back to the question in your answer. This helps to keep your ideas focused.

OVERALL COMMENT

This response would achieve a Level 1. The student has used evidence from the cartoon to explain how we can tell that it opposes the Treaty of Versailles. To develop the answer so that it would achieve Level 2, the student would have to use their own knowledge about the treaty to explain why people felt that it was too harsh on Germany.

OVER TO YOU

1. Review the sample answer:

   a highlight anywhere that the student used evidence from the source

   b underline the sentences where the student directly answers the question about how they knew the source opposes the Treaty of Versailles

2 **a** Now have a go at writing your own answer. You should spend around five minutes on this type of question.

   b Review your answer. Did you…

   ☐ use specific evidence from the source?

   ☐ use your own knowledge and give at least one example of the treaty terms and how it harmed Germany (and try to explain something other than the economic terms)? You could think about the military terms, the land Germany lost, or how the treaty affected German pride.

   ☐ make sure your answer is focused on the question by using the same wording in your answer?

   Go back to Chapters 2 and 3 to help refresh your knowledge of the Treaty of Versailles.

▶ **SOURCE B** *A British cartoon from 1919, showing Uncle Sam who represents the USA; a keystone is an important stone in a structure – without it the bridge is weak*

THE GAP IN THE BRIDGE.

▼ **SOURCE C** Adapted from a memo written by the British Foreign Secretary, Arthur Balfour, 15 March 1920; Balfour discusses the League and the problems they faced regarding reaching a settlement with Turkey:

The chief weapons of the League are Public Discussion, Investigation, Arbitration [diplomacy] and finally in the last resort Compulsion [meaning military action]. These are powerful weapons, but there are regions where nothing but force is understood, and where even force is useless if it isn't rapidly applied. It would seem that in parts of the world such as these the League can only be effective if there is a Great Power with a mandate [authority] through which the League can act. If no such Great Power can be found the League cannot be an effective substitute.

 2 Study **Sources B** and **C**. How useful are **Sources B** and **C** to a historian studying why the League of Nations failed to keep the peace? Explain your answer using **Sources B** and **C** and your contextual knowledge.

12 marks

Sample student answer

Taken together, the sources are useful as evidence of the issues faced by the League of Nations that led to its downfall. Source B suggests that the fact that the USA did not join the League of Nations was a massive issue. The cartoon shows that there is a 'keystone' missing from the bridge and that piece is the USA. The sign references the fact that the 'bridge', or the League, was designed by the President of the USA, and it is true that Woodrow Wilson suggested it in his Fourteen Points. Therefore, many people felt that if the country that invented the League wasn't even a member, then the League would not be as strong as it could have been. When the League was first introduced it was missing several powerful countries: the US Senate refused to allow the USA to join. Many questioned whether collective security could work, if important and key powers were missing. Therefore this source is useful as it identifies a key reason for the failure of the League to keep the peace – a lack of powerful countries.

The fact that the source is British could make it one-sided. The British view was that the League had no real power and so it wasn't taken seriously. It was seen as somewhere countries could discuss an issue, but no action would take place.

EXAMINER TIP

Here, the student has used evidence from the source and their own knowledge to explain how one source is useful, so this is a Level 2 answer so far.

EXAMINER TIP

Look at the key historical terms used as evidence; this shows that the student has good contextual knowledge.

EXAMINER TIP

Here, the student has identified an issue, but not really made it relevant to the question. Remember that the question wants you to be positive about the source; here the fact that the source is British and one-sided isn't necessarily a problem as it is useful for demonstrating how people in Britain, including Lloyd George, lacked faith in the League.

OVERALL COMMENT

This answer would achieve a low Level 3. It explains the use of one source, using factual knowledge to explain what the source is about. The student also tries to use the provenance, but doesn't make the link to the question clear enough to achieve a Level 4.

OVER TO YOU

1. Now have a go at the question yourself. You should spend around 15 minutes on this type of question. Read the overall comment carefully and think about what you would need to add or change in order to achieve a Level 4.

2   Review your answer. Did you…

☐ read the question carefully and make sure you addressed everything it asks you to do? For example, did you use both sources in your answer and explain them both?

☐ identify the reason for failure each source is about and use details (a quote from a written source or description of a visual source) as evidence to support your ideas?

☐ link each source to your own knowledge in order to explain why the League failed?

☐ identify what factor each source talks about, and then give an example or details about how this caused the League to fail using your own knowledge?

☐ use the information in the captions (provenance)?

Go back to pages 40–41 to help refresh your knowledge of the reasons why the League of Nations failed.

EXAMINER TIP

When analysing and evaluating a source it's a good idea to look at the provenance. This will help you decide how useful the source is – if it is one-sided or unreliable it may not be useful to a historian for the purpose stated in the question.

The 'write an account' question

 Write an account of how events in Abyssinia became an international crisis in the years 1934 to 1936.

8 marks

Sample student answer

The situation in Abyssinia became an international crisis because Mussolini invaded the capital, Addis Ababa, and during his invasion he used chemicals to terrorise people into surrendering. The fact that Mussolini was willing to act in an inhumane way made people question what other regulations he would ignore.

Another reason events in Abyssinia became an international crisis was because Britain and France were seen to undermine the League of Nations. The Hoare–Laval Plan was leaked by the press, exposing the fact that the foreign ministers of the two most powerful members of the League were willing to give in to Mussolini, by offering him land in Abyssinia in order to end the invasion. Although the plan was never realised, it led to international crisis – the League was meant to prevent war, yet key members were willing to ignore Mussolini's act of war in order to keep him as an ally against Hitler. This undermined the League, made it look weak, and led to crisis as people felt that they could no longer put their faith in collective security – each country wanted to look after their self interests and could not be relied upon to support others to prevent war.

OVERALL COMMENT

This answer achieves a Level 3. It is well focused on the question, by giving an explanation at the end of each point. To achieve a Level 4, the student would need to organise their answer – so that events flow in chronological order – and explain each stage of the crisis, showing how one event led to another, causing tension to grow.

OVER TO YOU

1   Have a go at answering the question yourself. Try to think about the other events that caused the crisis in Abyssinia in 1934–36: can you link the events to each other to show how one caused the next? You should spend around 10 minutes on your answer.

2   Review your answer. Did you…

- [ ] explain at least two events concerning Abyssinia that caused crisis in 1934–36?

- [ ] make sure that the events are dealt with in chronological order?

- [ ] make sure your answer is focused on the question by using the same wording in your answer?

- [ ] make links between each event to show how tension grew?

Go back to pages 36–39 to help refresh your knowledge of the Abyssinian crisis.

The 'how far do you agree' question

EXAM QUESTION 'Appeasement was the main reason for the outbreak of the Second World War.' How far do you agree with this statement? Explain your answer.

16 marks   SPaG 4 marks

EXAMINER TIP

Don't spend too long on an introduction as you're unlikely to pick up many marks in this section. However, in order to sustain your judgment throughout your answer, it is important to make your overall opinion clear from the start of your essay, like the student has done here. If you want to achieve a Level 4, it is important that your overall view is apparent all the way through your response.

EXAMINER TIP

Don't forget that you can pick up more marks here for showing the examiner that you can use spelling, punctuation and grammar correctly. It is worth factoring in some time to check your answer at the end. Make sure you write in paragraphs and that you use capital letters for proper nouns. Try to use historical terms — the glossary at the back of this book can help you become familiar with terms that could be useful in your exam.

Sample student answer

Although some historians disagree, it is my belief that appeasement was not the main reason for the outbreak of war, but it was a mistake as it allowed Hitler the time and confidence to prepare for war, so it was a contributing factor. I believe that the main cause of the Second World War was actually the Treaty of Versailles, as it was this that led to Hitler's aggressive foreign policy.

Hitler's foreign policy including taking Lebensraum or 'living space'. Germany had lost 10% of its land in the Treaty of Versailles, so Hitler and many of his supporters felt that they were entitled to reclaim it. Hitler was determined to take Lebensraum from Eastern European countries, which led to him invading places like Czechoslovakia and Poland. If it wasn't for the Treaty of Versailles taking land from Germany, Hitler may not have invaded other countries, so there would have been no need for appeasement.

However, reclaiming the land Germany lost to Poland in 1919, by invading it in 1939, was the spark that led to war. Britain and France had signed agreements saying that they would protect Poland, so when Hitler invaded they had to act and this was the main reason for the outbreak of the Second World War.

It was also the Treaty of Versailles that led to Britain following the policy of appeasement towards Hitler. For example, when Hitler remilitarised the Rhineland in 1936 the British response was that it was fine to do this, as it was reasonable for Hitler to 'march into his own back garden'. British politicians believed that the terms of the Treaty of Versailles were too harsh and so it was fine to let Hitler get away with breaking the terms of the treaty. Similarly, when Hitler achieved Anschluss with Austria in 1938, Britain did not act because it believed that the treaty had been too harsh by preventing two countries with a shared heritage from uniting. Anschluss was therefore ignored, and an opportunity to stop Hitler on his path to war was missed.

EXAMINER TIP

The candidate has used lots of good, detailed factual knowledge to support their ideas. They are also using historical terminology like 'Lebensraum' which may help improve their SPaG mark.

EXAMINER TIP

Look at how the student links their ideas back to the question at the end of each paragraph. This helps them to make sure that they are explaining their answer rather than simply giving a narrative of events.

However, the statement is true in so much as appeasement contributed to the outbreak of war. Appeasement meant that Hitler grew confident and took greater risks. For example, when he remilitarised the Rhineland in 1936, Hitler's advisers warned him that if he was challenged Germany was not strong enough to win. If British or French soldiers had acted in any way to stop Hitler he would have had to withdraw. However, because they did not, Hitler was able to remilitarise and realised that he could break international law (the Treaty of Versailles) without punishment. This meant that he was able to go onto achieve Anschluss, and when he was once more appeased he went on to the Sudetenland and then Czechoslovakia. Therefore appeasement was a factor in causing the war because those who appeased Hitler missed opportunities to stop him when he was weak, which meant that he was able to grow more confident and to become more powerful.

However, my reason for questioning that appeasement was the main reason for the outbreak of war is that without the other factors like the harsh terms of the Treaty of Versailles, the Depression or Hitler's aggressive foreign policy, there would have been no need for Britain and France to have followed the policy of appeasement. Therefore, I believe that the harsh nature of the Treaty of Versailles was the only reason the policy of appeasement was followed in the first place. Without the harsh treaty, which even David Lloyd George and Woodrow Wilson had said was too harsh when they signed it, Hitler would have had no reason for developing a foreign policy which could only be achieved with aggression, invasion of other countries, and ultimately war, and it was only the British feeling that Germany should be allowed to act this way because the treaty had been unfair that prevented them from acting earlier.

EXAMINER TIP

It's important that you explain both the factor in the statement and others. Look at how the candidate has explained the policy of appeasement, even though they disagree with the statement overall.

EXAMINER TIP

If you have time, it's a good idea to try to explain more than one piece of evidence for each side of the argument. Here the candidate has only explained one reason appeasement can be seen as a cause of the war. Adding a second would strengthen the answer.

EXAMINER TIP

Here the candidate has come to a very clear final judgment, evaluating the weaknesses of other factors to explain why one reason is more significant than the others.

OVERALL COMMENT

This answer would achieve a Level 4. The student has explained why the statement is true, but has also analysed other factors, and has a clear and sustained judgment that runs all the way through the answer.

To strengthen the response the student could add further evidence explaining how appeasement led to the outbreak of war. This would achieve a higher mark within Level 4.

OVER TO YOU

1 Explanation is the key to getting a good level in this type of question. Go through the answer and underline each time the student explains by linking their ideas back to the question.

2 Create a flashcard summarising the evidence and arguments that you could use if you were asked this question in the exam.

3 Now that you've read an example of a top level response, revisit one of the 'How far do you agree' essays that you've written in the past (there are lots of examples in this book) and see if you can improve it.

4 Review your answer. Did you...

☐ include both sides of the argument

☐ mention specific evidence – events, dates etc. – to support your ideas?

☐ link back to the question at the end of each paragraph to help you to explain your ideas?

☐ contain accurate spelling, punctuation and grammar?

☐ include a clear judgement that runs all the way through your answer?

Go back to Chapters 7–9 to help refresh your knowledge of the causes of the Second World War.

EXAMINER TIP

Be careful in the exam; read the questions carefully and make sure that you always answer what is asked, rather than a question you've revised.

The answers provided here are examples, based on the information provided in the Recap sections of this Revision Guide. There may be other factors which are relevant to each question, and you should draw on as much of your own knowledge as possible to give detailed and precise answers. There are also many ways of answering exam questions (for example, of structuring an essay). However, these exemplar answers should provide a good starting point.

Chapter 1   Page 13

WRITE AN ACCOUNT

You should produce your own set of revision flashcards for this activity.

SOURCE ANALYSIS

a   You might circle words like Source A; opposes; Clemenceau; aims; explain; contextual knowledge.

b   A good answer could include evidence from the cartoon, such as Clemenceau being shown as a fierce tiger, killing a startled eagle; the eagle was a symbol used to represent Germany before and during the First World War. Own knowledge could include details about how Clemenceau wanted a harsh treaty, in comparison to the other members of the Big Three who wanted a fair treaty so that future war would be averted.

Chapter 2   Page 15

HOW FAR DO YOU AGREE?

Damage to pride: not being allowed to join the League of Nations

Economic damage: loss of land meant loss of resources, e.g. coal in the Saar; loss of military meant fewer jobs in the armed forces and in factories making tanks etc.

Military loss: reductions to the army and navy; no tanks, submarines or air force; number of battleships limited; demilitarisation of the Rhineland

Territorial loss: Polish Corridor; Danzig; the Saar; loss of colonies

HOW FAR DO YOU AGREE?

The categories you came up with in your answer to the 'How far do you agree?' activity above can be used as evidence when completing your essay plan. You will need to make sure you explain the impact on Germany – for example, you could agree with the statement because the reparations were humiliating for Germany. They weakened the country and left it unable to function, especially having just fought in the First World War.

Chapter 3   Page 17

HOW FAR DO YOU AGREE?

a   You should produce your own ranking line and explanations for this activity.

b   You should write out what you think the three most important factors are, in order of importance.

c   You should produce your own fact sheet for this activity.

d   A good essay might include:
   • reasons the Big Three disagreed, such as Wilson's desire for freedom of the seas versus Lloyd George's desire for Naval Supremacy; or Clemenceau's need for reparations versus Lloyd George's aim to keep Germany strong so that they could trade
   • other reasons the Big Three might have been dissatisfied with the Treaty, such as: the armistice, which meant that some ideas had already been accepted and the Big Three could not change these; and time restraints, which meant that the Big Three had to hurry to make the agreement because Europe (especially the Austrio-Hungarian Empire) was collapsing around them and a resolution was needed quickly so that people could get the help they needed after the war – this meant that the Big Three had to hurry to conclude the treaty and had less time to explore different ideas.

Page 19

SOURCE ANALYSIS

The plate is British – there is an image of St Paul's Cathedral on it and it is positive about the Treaty of Versailles, saying that it is a 'victory'. When adding your own knowledge you could include details such as: some people in Britain felt like this and greeted Lloyd George as a hero on his return from Paris because they agreed with terms, such as Germany losing land (for example the Polish Corridor).

SOURCE ANALYSIS

a   The source criticises the treaty for:
   • failing to help rebuild the economies of Europe (Lloyd George would agree with this because he was worried that the German economy was crippled and would not be able to trade)
   • a lack of action to help relationships with the defeated countries (Lloyd George and Wilson would agree with this because Germany was not allowed to join the League of Nations, and both men feared that Germany would be angry about the treaty which would lead to war again in the future)
   • the fact that the new countries in Europe would be unstable (Wilson would agree with this because many countries in Eastern Europe grouped together different ethnic groups, rather than allowing complete self-determination; this led to problems in areas such as Upper Silesia where Poles and Germans were mixed)
   • the fact that the war cost places like France a lot and the treaty would not address this (Clemenceau and France, as well as some British people, would agree with this because they felt that reparations would have to be much higher in order to rebuild the regions of France which had been destroyed in the war)

b   The source was written by esteemed British economist Keynes, who was an expert on economics and therefore had authority when commenting on the economic impact of the treaty. He was also present at the conference, so understood what happened and what the terms were. However, he was British so was likely to share some of the concerns that other British people had, such as Lloyd George's concerns that Germany would be left too poor to be able to trade.

c   Use the sources and the facts you have added to the table in part **b** to help you answer this exam question.

Page 21

SOURCE ANALYSIS

a   A good answer will include: the fact that the treaty was a Diktat accepted by the November Criminals; the humiliation of the war guilt clause; economic sanctions leaving Germany unable to recover and causing unrest such as the crisis in the Ruhr, 1923.

b   **Short-term impacts** would include Germany not being able to recover after the war; families starving; the Ruhr crisis leading to hyperinflation. **Long-term impacts** would include having to take out loans from the USA which made Germany vulnerable when the Depression hit in 1929.

c   The cartoon criticises the November Criminals as it shows a German soldier having been stabbed in the back – referring to the 'stab in the back' myth. This was the idea that many Germans felt that they had been winning the war and therefore those who surrendered had betrayed them, leaving Germany to suffer under terms of the Treaty of Versailles, including the steep reparations that crippled the country.

HOW FAR DO YOU AGREE?

A good answer will explain the impact the financial terms had on Germany, for example: the reparations, set at £6,600 million in 1921, weakened Germany; Germany had to rebuild after the war, which had already devastated the economy (people were starving by the end of the war), so it could not afford to pay the reparations. You could link this to the crisis in the Ruhr, when France invaded Germany to take goods when the reparation payments were not made. German workers were then paid to strike, leading to hyperinflation which destroyed the German economy, forced it to take loans from the USA, and encouraged Hitler and the Nazis to attempt to overthrow the government in the Munich Putsch. You should also explain the impact of other terms, such as the loss of land like the Saar that left German people living in new countries at a time when many other nations were hostile to Germany; military restrictions such as the limit of the army to 100,000 men and no conscriptions, which left

Germany feeling vulnerable to attack; or the war guilt clause which meant Germany had to accept responsibility for starting the war. You will also need an overall judgment: historians tend to agree that it was the war guilt clause that was most hated in Germany as it was used to justify every other punishment – if the war was Germany's fault then the allies were right to punish them. Alternatively, you could argue that even David Lloyd George and Woodrow Wilson felt that the economic sanctions were too harsh, with Lloyd George fearing the collapse of Anglo-German trade and Wilson fearing Germany seeking revenge and starting another war.

Page 23

HOW FAR DO YOU AGREE?

a The order of the countries will be your own.

b You should produce your own explanation for this activity.

WRITE AN ACCOUNT

a The problems caused by the treaties could include: the Treaties of St Germain and Neuilly leading to economic collapse in Austria and Hungary; the Treaty of Sevres leading to revolution in Turkey; the Treaty of Versailles leaving Germany financially crippled and feeling vulnerable because of the military restrictions.

b You account could include: resentment towards the treaty leading to protests, which led to the government being overthrow; how this lead to a new treaty – the Treaty of Lausanne, which showed that the treaties were impossible to enforce, undermined the peace treaties, and showed people like Hitler and Mussolini that they could get away with ignoring the treaties.

Page 25

WRITE AN ACCOUNT

a You should produce your own flashcards for this activity.

b Your answer could include points such as: Poland was left with enemies all around and borders that were hard to defend; German nationals found themselves living in other countries, such as the Sudetenland in Czechoslovakia and the Polish Corridor – they faced persecution and resented being ruled by a different nationality.

SOURCE ANALYSIS

a A good answer will use details from the source, such as the obvious pain that the character representing Germany is in, or the fact that the 'pill' is too big for Germany to physically swallow. You should also link this to your own knowledge to explain why people in Germany felt this way. For example, you could explain that having their army reduced to 100,000 left Germany feeling vulnerable, or that they felt the war guilt clause was unfair as lots of countries arguing over empires and forming alliances was the cause of the war.

b A good answer will explain what the two sources are useful for. Source B shows how the people in Germany reacted by protesting against the treaty, which could be linked to the idea of the November Criminals or the 'stabbed in the back' idea. Source C is useful as it shows the resentment people felt towards the treaty and suggests that Germany had things taken from it unfairly. This could be linked to your own knowledge of the land that Germany lost, such as the Saar or the Polish Corridor, that it felt was rightfully German. The provenance of the sources should also be considered, so the fact that both sources were created shortly after the signing of the treaty make them useful for the immediate reaction, but a historian may want to consider other sources to examine the long-term impact and reaction.

Chapter 4   Page 27

HOW FAR DO YOU AGREE?

a **Strengths** could include: the number of members who could put economic sanctions on an aggressor; efforts to make things fair, such as the unanimous vote; members such as Britain and France who had proven to the world that they were powerful by winning the war and having huge empires. **Weaknesses** could include: lack of the USA, Germany and Russia; no army; unfair that the Council could veto; complex organisation.

b Use your answers to part **a** to help you plan your essay. A good essay will include an introduction, which will set out your overall judgement, followed by two sides of the argument, and then a conclusion bringing your ideas together and focusing on your overall judgement.

SOURCE ANALYSIS

a Key features of the cartoon include: a muzzle (a device put over the mouth of an animal to stop it from biting/attacking people); a fierce-looking dog labelled 'the dog of war'; the label on the muzzle that reads 'the League of Nations'; the caption of the cartoon, which has a question mark.

b Your answer could include statements such as: 'I can tell that the source criticises the League because of the question mark in the caption. This suggests that the creator is not convinced that the League will successfully stop war. Some people felt that the League would not be able to stop war because they did not have an army – this was later proved in events such as in Vilna in 1920 and in Corfu in 1923.

Page 29

WRITE AN ACCOUNT

Use the following letters to create your acronym: I or L (International **L**abour Organisation); R (Commission for **R**efugees); S (Commission for **S**lavery); E or F (**E**conomic and **F**inancial committee); C or T (Organisation for **C**ommunication and **T**ransport); H (Health

Organisation); O (Permanent Central **O**pium Board). For example, you could remember the agencies using the acronym: **HORSE IT**.

HOW FAR DO YOU AGREE?

Successes could include: Improving working conditions – reducing the death rate of workers on the Tanganyika railway, freeing slaves in Sierra Leone; Healthcare and curing disease – helping in Turkish refugee camps.

Failures could include: Improving working conditions – failure to stop under-fourteens from working; Healthcare and curing disease – some countries not supporting the ban on opium, fighting leprosy.

Page 31

WRITE AN ACCOUNT

a The League's decision was accepted in all three events.

b Vilna – Britain and France undermined the League; Upper Silesia – Poland refused to accept the result of the plebiscite and the resulting compromise was messy and left both countries feeling that they had been treated unfairly; Corfu – Mussolini was powerful so the League, without an army of its own, had no power over him; Bulgaria – Greece claimed that the result illustrated that it was one rule for big, powerful countries like Italy in the Corfu crisis; and another for smaller countries such as themselves.

c Use your ideas for part **b** to answer the question. Try to deal with events in chronological order, briefly describe what happened, but also explain what led to the League's failure in each one. For example, when explaining the crisis in Vilna, you could describe what happened (Polish forces took over the Lithuanian capital Vilna) and that the League failed to act. This was because it wanted to keep Poland strong, and so ignored this clearly aggressive act. This undermined the League, as one of its aims was to keep peace, but it was prepared to turn a blind eye to aggression if it suited the League's interests.

HOW FAR DO YOU AGREE?

You should produce your own revision flashcard for this activity.

Chapter 5   Page 33

SOURCE ANALYSIS

a Relevant evidence from Source A could include: a radical and complete change in European politics; transforming the relations between the former antagonists; attempt to base politics on the principle of mutual friendship and trust. Source B shows the foreign ministers of Germany and France working together, which was important as the countries had been sworn enemies before, during and after the First World War.

b It was important that the League was not involved in these treaties because it should have been leading the way on international treaties that helped preserve peace – however it wasn't doing this, which damaged its reputation.

c Usefulness could include that the sources highlight important failures of the League by demonstrating the importance of treaties with which they were not involved. For example, the fact that Source A was written as a speech given at the Noble Peace Prize ceremony means that it would celebrate the significance of these treaties, but it might also therefore exaggerate it. The fact that Nansen worked with the League could make it even more useful; he would not have wanted to undermine the League, so if he thought something it was not involved in really was significant, then that is important. Source B is from a French magazine, arguably the French are trying to glorify their involvement in the Kellogg-Briand Pact, which may exaggerate how important it was.

Chapter 6   Page 35

WRITE AN ACCOUNT

a **Great Depression**: caused the crisis by giving Japan the need to invade Manchuria for resources; countries could not afford to send an army so the League could not force Japan to withdraw; **League did not have its own army**: the League could not force Japan to do anything; when it ignored the League's condemnation the League was powerless to stop the invasion; **Membership of the League**: the fact that the USA, who were Japan's biggest trading partner, was not a member of the League meant that economic sanctions wouldn't have had much impact on them, and the lack of Russia was important as it shared a border with China and could have intervened much more easily than European powers; **Japan undermining the League**: Japan was a member of the Permanent Council – when they ignored the League and left it undermined its authority.

b Your summary/plan could include: the Depression – caused Japan's economic decline as it could not trade silk, so needed to invade for resources; the Mukden incident – an explosion on a Japanese-owned railway – Japan blamed China and retaliated by invading; the League became involved – moral condemnation was issued, but had no effect; the League could not use economic sanctions (due to Depression) and had no army; Lytton Report – took too long, Japan ignored it and left the League, so the League was made to look weak.

HOW FAR DO YOU AGREE?

The League's reputation remained intact because many people did not feel that Asia was in its sphere of influence; people still had faith that the League would be effective if a problem like this one happened in Europe. However, the League's reputation in the eyes of more militaristic countries, like Italy or Germany, was damaged. They concluded that the League

might not have the will or resources to oppose their ambitions.

Page 37

HOW FAR DO YOU AGREE?

a You should produce your own set of revision flashcards for this activity.

b A good answer plan will include how the Abyssinian crisis undermined the League. This could include the Hoare-Laval Pact, ineffective trade sanctions, or the failure to close the Suez Canal showing that leading members were prepared to undermine the League, making it look weak. To explain that other factors also contributed you could include in your plan the long-term issues such as the League's inability to punish strong countries, as seen in the Corfu and Vilna crises of the 1920s, the lack of countries like the USA and USSR, or the Manchurian crisis. Your overall judgement could show links between the factors, such as Mussolini being shown he could act as he pleased with no repercussions, leading him to invade Abyssinia, or you could consider what had changed by the 1930s – the Great Depression had hit, so leaders like Mussolini were more likely to be aggressive, and countries like Britain and France could not afford to intervene as trade sanctions/ use of force would be too expensive.

c Use your plan to write your answer. Try to explain at least two factors and link these back to the question to help focus your answer.

SOURCE ANALYSIS

a The cartoon is about the Hoare-Laval Pact, which was agreed during the Abyssinian crisis. Facts about this event could include: Hoare and Laval were the British and French foreign ministers; they planned to give parts of Abyssinia to Mussolini; the plan was leaked to the press; people were outraged by the plan.

b It made the League look bad because it showed that the most powerful countries in the League could undermine its aims.

c A good answer will include detail from the source, such as the weak and feeble-looking woman used to represent the League, or Mussolini's description of the League ('contemptible', 'can do nothing'), as well as factual evidence that proves that the League failed, such as the Hoare-Laval Pact or the League's failure to stop trading important war materials such as coal (as this might have led to unemployment in Britain).

Page 39

WRITE AN ACCOUNT

You should produce your own set of flashcards for this activity.

HOW FAR DO YOU AGREE?

a For example: their desire to keep Mussolini as an ally against Hitler, leading to them not

closing the Suez Canal during the Abyssinian crisis. This meant that the League failed because: the world saw two of the permanent members of the Council putting their own interests over the principles of collective security and striving for peace; this undermined the League, made it look weak, and meant that countries lost all respect for it as a peace keeping organisation.

b The Depression: it made countries desperate, which meant they more likely to attack others, e.g. Japan invaded Manchuria because it needed natural resources; Hitler left the disarmament conference because rearming meant jobs for the people of Germany; Mussolini invaded Abyssinia to distract the people of Italy from domestic problems; other countries could not afford to lend the League their armies and did not want to inflict economic sanctions that would affect their own economies, for example Britain did not ban the sale of coal to Italy during the Abyssinian crisis.

c Long-term structural weaknesses could include: lack of important countries like the USA – caused problems e.g. during the Manchurian crisis as economic sanctions were useless since the USA was Japan's main trade partner; lack of an army – Japan could ignore the League's demands to leave China without fear of further action; Britain and France had too much power in the League – see guidance on part **a** for examples you could use for this point.

Page 40

HOW FAR DO YOU AGREE?

a **Depression**: countries were more likely to invade others, for example Japan invaded Manchuria because it was rich in natural resources. Use this example as a model for the other points.

b **Depression**: this meant that the League failed because it was meant to ensure peace, but countries were attacking others to make money. Use this example as a model for the other points.

c A good answer will explain a couple of reasons the Depression led to the failure of the League, such as: the way countries like Italy, Japan and Germany were more likely to invade others in order to make money; or how the Depression limited the reaction of other countries and their ability to support the League against aggressors, such as the failure of sanctions during the Abyssinian crisis because it would mean a loss of trade for Britain and France. Your answer should also include other factors. Chose your answers to parts **a** and **b** that you are most confident about explaining. For example, because the USA wasn't a member of the League, trade sanctions against Japan during the Manchurian crisis were useless. The USA was Japan's main trade partner, so the threat of losing trade with members of the League like Britain and France was not a deterrent. Finally, you need to consider an overall judgement.

Chapter 7   Page 42

SOURCE ANALYSIS

a 1 is in Hitler's hand; 2 is the front of row of 'people' waiting; 3 is behind the figure on the left; 4 is at the end of the line of 'ghosts'; 5 is on the left.

b They are towards the back because Hitler will invade in the east first, but the cartoonist is warning that he will eventually get to Britain and the USA.

c The cartoon is critical because it suggests that Hitler has a whole host of German-speaking people in different parts of Europe and the world that he can argue should be united under his leadership. The cartoonist is critical of his own leaders' policies and suspicious of Hitler's foreign policy ambitions in September 1938 with regard to the Sudetenland Germans. If the Sudetenland is conceded then Hitler will have many other German-speaking groups with which to haunt the West.

d The source is about Hitler's aim of overturning the Treaty of Versailles and rearming Germany.

e Sources A and B are useful because they show that an important cause of the Second World War was Hitler's foreign policy. This was driven in turn by his desire to unite all German-speaking people, overturn Versailles, and rearm Germany after the First World War. All of these points are made in Source A, and since this was written in 1925 it shows how long he had held these desires for. At that time he was in prison and could not have anticipated the Depression and its impact on Germany. He was merely voicing the concerns of a former German soldier. Source B reflects the Allied response to Hitler's foreign policy, which was appeasement, and by 1938 cartoonists such as Low were expressing commonly held views that appeasement was not working – on the contrary it was fuelling Hitler's demands.

Page 45

HOW FAR DO YOU AGREE?

a **Hitler's aim(s)** – Dollfuss: uniting German speakers; Saar: uniting German speakers; Rearmament: re-establishing the German army, but this also allows him to achieve his other aims; Anglo-German Naval Agreement: rearmament

b **Term(s) violated** – Dollfuss: *Anschluss* forbidden; Saar: technically none – the Saar was put under control of the League for 15 years, after which they could and did vote on which country to be part of; Rearmament/ Anglo-German Naval Agreement: Germany was only allowed 100,000 men, no conscription, no tanks/aeroplanes, 6 battleships and a navy of 15,000 men

SOURCE ANALYSIS

a Labels could include: the large man representing Britain – it has the strongest and most developed navy so the figure is large; the boy representing Germany because they are being allowed to build a new navy – so it is young, like a child; a man sulking, representing France, who was fearful of Germany being allowed to rearm as they had attacked France before; sailors' uniforms to show that the source is about the Anglo-German naval agreement in which Germany was allowed to build ships and recruit sailors; the year (1935) as that was when the Anglo-German naval agreement was signed; the text – warning that the German navy will get bigger because many felt that Britain was wrong to sign this agreement as it violated the terms of the Treaty of Versailles and because people were fearful as Hitler had already announced that he was rebuilding his army.

b From the cartoon: Germany is saying that they will ignore the agreement if they feel they need to, France is not happy, Germany looks quite arrogant. From contextual knowledge: Britain gave Germany permission to break the terms of the treaty which persuaded him that he could get away with more and more – he'd already got away with rebuilding his army, now he could do the same with his navy.

Chapter 8   Page 47

SOURCE ANALYSIS

a The goose has a laurel leaf in its beak; the Nazi flags in the background suggest that people were in favour of Hitler's actions; the Goose has a sign saying 'Pax Germanica' – German peace.

b The goose has weapons; the goose step is a military march; the goose is stamping on a torn up Locarno Treaty which had promised nations would work together for peace.

c Use your answer from part **b** for source detail. For contextual knowledge you could include: remilitarisation was against the Treaty of Versailles; Hitler needed to protect his western border if he was to invade for *Lebensraum* in the east; Hitler knew he was violating the treaty and was ready for opposition.

WRITE AN ACCOUNT

a You could include words like: Treaty of Versailles (because that was when Germany was forced to demilitarise the Rhineland); *Lebensraum* (Hitler needed to remilitarise to protect his western borders so that he could take *Lebensraum* in the east); Franco-Soviet pact (because Hitler used this as an excuse, claiming that France and the USSR were uniting against him); 1936 (troops entered the Rhineland); reaction (people gave the troops flowers – Hitler could remilitarise because people wanted him to).

b Start with why Hitler wanted to remilitarise the Rhineland (violate the treaty, protect his western border so he could advance in the east) and then explain how he achieved this (warnings from his ministers, advice to the army on what to do if they were challenged, marching the soldiers in, the reaction he faced).

Page 49

WRITE AN ACCOUNT

a In your timeline you could include: Before 1934 – Austria ruled Germany for 600 years; 1933 – Hitler comes to power, one of his promises is Anschluss; 1934 – Hitler tries to take Austria, Mussolini prevents him; 1938 – Nazi plot discovered by Austrian police, Schuschnigg meets with Hitler and gives Nazis positions in government, Seyss-Inquart appointed and given full control of Austrian police, Schuschnigg plans a plebiscite, Hitler demands the plebiscite is delayed, Schuschnigg is forced to resign, Seyss-Inquart is made Chancellor, he claims there is chaos and asks for Hitler's help to return order; 12 March 1938 – Nazi troops enter Austria, 10 April 1938 – plebiscite is held, Austria and Germany unite.

b *Anschluss* was important to Hitler because he was Austrian; the two countries had a shared history; Hitler could now swell his army with Austrian ranks; this was the first time his actions involved another country so he was really testing how much he could get away with. *Anschluss* gave Hitler great confidence that the allies would not act when he turned his attention to *Lebensraum* in the east.

c Use the events from your timeline and make sure you explain what issues they caused. For example, the Dolfuss affair in 1934 led to crisis because the Austrian Chancellor was assassinated and it looked like Hitler would invade. Tension grew as Mussolini moved his troops to the Austrian border.

Page 51

SOURCE ANALYSIS

a The wolf is Germany; the two men in the left hand corner are Britain and France; the see-through man is the USA.

b The source suggests Hitler wants Czechoslovakia because it will: make his army proud (prestige); prepare Germany for war (e.g. there were natural resources and factories – like the Skoda factory – that could help make weapons) which would help them in a war against Britain and France.

c Source A is useful because it suggests that Hitler took Czechoslovakia because he could – there is no reaction from Britain and France. The cartoon suggests that the Munich Conference was a mistake. However, because the source is Russian it may be biased – they were very concerned that Hitler was creeping towards them in the east. This cartoon foreshadows the Nazi-Soviet Pact that the USSR signed because they felt threatened and thought it would protect them (for a little while).

Source B is useful for explaining the material gains – how Czechoslovakia made Hitler stronger and ready for war. The fact that it is British could be surprising as it is a member of Chamberlain's own party, suggesting that appeasement/the Munich Conference could be a mistake, but we know that other politicians, like Churchill, did feel this way at this time.

Page 53

SOURCE ANALYSIS

a The hat and umbrella, in contrast to Mars' weapons, show that Chamberlain is trying to use diplomacy to deal with Hitler – he is a man of peace and is trying to avoid war through the policy of appeasement.

b Chamberlain is shown bravely facing the God of War, he looks strong and determined. Contextual knowledge could include any of the arguments that support appeasement, such as Chamberlain wanting to avoid war because his own son had died in the First World War and he wanted to avoid others going through this devastation. The source is from October 1938 so will be about the Sudeten Crisis, the Munich Conference and the 'peace in our time' speech.

HOW FAR DO YOU AGREE?

On your flashcards try to use mnemonics, acronyms, colour and/or images to help you remember the information.

Chapter 9   Page 55

HOW FAR DO YOU AGREE?

a Your timeline could include the following events: 1933 – Hitler leaves the disarmament conference; 1934 – Dolfuss affair, Hitler attempts Anschluss; 1935 – (January) Saar plebiscite, (March) rearmament announced, (June) Anglo-German Naval Agreement; 1936 – (July) Hitler tests his weapons in the Spanish Civil War, (October) Rome-Berlin Axis agreed; 1937 – Japanese full scale invasion of China; 1938 – (March) Hitler sends troops into Austria, (September) Sudeten Crisis, Munich Conference, (October) Nazi troops occupy the Sudetenland; 1939 – (March) Nazi troops invade the rest of Czechoslovakia, (May) Pact of Steel signed, (August) Nazi-Soviet Pact signed, (September) Hitler invades Poland, Britain and France declare war on Germany.

b **Hitler's foreign policy**: leaving the disarmament conference (rearmament); remilitarisation of the Rhineland (against the Treaty of Versailles); *Anschluss* (Greater Germany and uniting German-speaking people); Sudetenland and Poland

Treaty of Versailles: Anglo-German Naval Agreement (Britain felt that Germany had been left defenceless in Versailles, so it should be allowed to ignore some of the terms about their navy); remilitarisation of the Rhineland (Britain felt this term had been too harsh so allowed Germany to

remilitarise); *Anschluss* (Britain felt that the two nations were basically one anyway, so this term had been too harsh and Anschluss should be allowed)

Depression: Hitler became Chancellor (people supported him because he promised to make Germany strong again); Munich Conference (one of the reasons Chamberlain appeased Hitler was because he could not afford to go to war)

Appeasement: remilitarisation of the Rhineland (opportunities to stop Hitler while he was still weak were missed); Munich Conference (Sudetenland given to Hitler even though he had little claim on it – led to invasion of Czechoslovakia)

Nazi-Soviet Pact: Munich Conference (alienated Stalin and pushed him towards an alliance with Hitler); invasion of Poland (Hitler no longer faced a war on two fronts, so felt confident he could invade).

c The Nazi-Soviet Pact led to war because it meant that Hitler could take Poland without facing a war on two fronts. After the invasion of Czechoslovakia, Britain and France had promised to support Poland if Hitler invaded, so when he did they were forced to act. This was the short-term cause of war. Other factors could include: appeasement (Britain and France could have prevented the rise of Hitler when he was still weak, such as when he remilitarised the Rhineland, but instead they appeased him which gave him confidence to carry on his road to war); Hitler's foreign policy (for example *Lebensraum* – taking land such as the Sudetenland, Czechoslovakia and Poland – meant that he would invade other countries which was an act of war); Treaty of Versailles (this was very harsh and meant that some people felt sympathy towards what Hitler was trying to achieve).

Page 57

WRITE AN ACCOUNT

a The Great Depression meant that Hitler came to power, was keen to invade other places and other countries were hesitant to take action because they could not afford a war or to lose potential allies.

The weakness and collapse of the League of Nations meant Hitler (and Mussolini) knew they faced little punishment/challenge when invading other countries.

American isolationism meant economic sanctions did not work as countries could still trade with the USA; the USA would not get involved when Hitler invaded other places, so he was more confident that he could do as he pleased.

Fear of Communism meant countries wanted to keep Hitler as their ally; they felt that the USSR was their biggest threat, so let Hitler get away with his actions. They also treated Stalin with contempt, so he chose to ally with Hitler in the Nazi-Soviet Pact which led to Hitler's invasion of Poland and war.

Chamberlain: appeased Hitler as he did not

want war (his son had been killed in the First World War and Britain's army was not ready to fight in the 1930s); this meant that valuable opportunities to stop Hitler when he was still weak (such as his remilitarisation of the Rhineland) were missed.

Stalin: agreed to the Nazi-Soviet Pact even though he was enemies with Hitler; this meant Hitler could invade Poland without facing a war on two fronts and this was the spark that started the Second World War.

Hitler: his aggressive foreign policy meant that he would take *Lebensraum*, which meant he would have to invade countries such as Czechoslovakia and Poland, an act of war that other countries could not ignore.

b For each person or issue, think carefully about what they did/what happened and how this led to war. There is no 'correct' answer – this task is about you explaining your ideas. Examples could include the Treaty of Versailles leading to Chamberlain's policy of appeasement; the Depression leading to the collapse of the League; Mussolini linking to Hitler as his invasion of Abyssinia distracted Britain and France while Hitler remilitarised the Rhineland.

c Look back at the timeline you created for part **a** of the 'How far do you agree?' activity on page 55. This will help you decide what to include. A good answer might include detail such as:

Hitler came to power in 1933, after the Depression left people in Germany desperate. He promised to make Germany great again by taking *Lebensraum* in the east.

Hitler started rearming and in 1934 announced that he was reintroducing conscription. This gave him the power to invade other countries.

In 1936, Hitler remilitarised the Rhineland. Britain saw no need to stop Hitler 'marching into his own back garden' so did not act. They failed to stop Hitler when he was still weak, because of appeasement.

1938 – *Anschluss* gave Hitler the strength of the Austrian army.

1938 – Munich Conference allowed Hitler to take the Sudetenland and then the rest of Czechoslovakia (1939); this was the first time he took an area/country that he had no real claim on. It also alienated Stalin.

1939 – Nazi-Soviet Pact meant Hitler would not face a war on two fronts, so he could invade Poland. Britain and France had agreed to protect Poland, so were forced to declare war.

HOW FAR DO YOU AGREE?

The guidance for part **c** for the 'Write an account' activity above gives examples of the events from the 1930s and how they led to war in 1939. You can use these to choose which events you would include on each side of your answer and to think about how to explain their significance/impact.

abdicate to give up the throne of a country

Anschluss union between Germany and Austria

appeasement policy of giving someone what they want in the hope of avoiding war

armistice initial agreement signed to stop fighting during a war; countries then work out a treaty of peace

Assembly a group of powerful countries which ran the League of Nations; Britain, France, Italy and Japan were permanent members and other countries were elected to serve for a term

the 'Big Three' (or the 'Big Four') representatives of the most powerful victorious countries who met at the Paris Peace Conference to decide how to treat the countries that had lost the war; consists of Britain, France and the USA (and Italy)

collective security working together to keep the peace

conscription compulsory military service

Council members of the League of Nations who met once a year to discuss and vote on matters of international importance

covenant an agreement; the Covenant of the League of Nations set up what the League was and what members could expect to happen under it

demilitarise to remove all military (weapons and troops) from an area

Diktat a forced treaty; Germany called the Treaty of Versailles a 'Diktat' or 'dictated peace'

empire a group of countries or states that are owned and ruled by one country

foreign minister a politician responsible for a country's relationship with other countries

hyperinflation when money becomes worthless

isolationism a policy in which a country does not get involved in foreign affairs

mandate a former colony (part of an empire) that was assigned to the League of Nations to be governed, until it was ready to look after itself

Paris Peace Conference meeting held at the Palace of Versailles in France at the end of the First World War, to decide how to punish the countries that had lost the war

Permanent Court of International Justice an international law court set up by the League of Nations

plebiscite when the people of a country, not just politicians, vote on a matter

propaganda using the media to persuade people to think a certain way

remilitarisation rebuilding stores of weapons and troops

reparations money paid as compensation to people or a country that has been harmed

self-determination the idea that countries should be allowed to govern themselves rather than being in an empire

Stresa Front an agreement made in 1935 between Italy, France and Britain, declaring that they would unite against Hitler

treaty a formal, legal agreement

veto the right to reject a proposal